THE PHYSICS OF DANCE

THE PHYSICS OF DANCE

Kenneth Laws

Dickinson College

photographs by Martha Swope

SCHIRMER BOOKS
A Division of Macmillan, Inc.
NEW YORK
Collier Macmillan Publishers
LONDON

Schirmer Books
A Division of Macmillan, Inc.
866 Third Avenue, New York, N.Y. 10022

Collier Macmillan Canada, Inc.

Human figure drawings by Sandra Kopell

Library of Congress Catalog Number: 83-20462

Schirmer Books Paperback Edition 1986

Printed in the United States of America

printing number hardcover
1 2 3 4 5 6 7 8 9 10

printing number paperback
1 2 3 4 5 6 7 8 9 10

Library of Congress Cataloging in Publication Data

Laws, Kenneth.
  The physics of dance.

  Includes index.
  1. Dancing—Physiological aspects. 2. Ballet dancing
—Physiological aspects. 3. Human mechanics. 4. Bio-
physics. I. Title.
QP310.D35L39   1984   792.8'01   83-20462
ISBN 0-02-872030-X
ISBN 0-02-873360-6 (pbk.)

To Lisa de Ribère—
whose belief and encouragement pervade these pages.

Contents

FOREWORD   xi

PREFACE   xiii
   The Artists   xiv

1 INTRODUCTION   1
   The Role of Physical Analysis   1
   Physics and Dance   4

2 BALANCE   11
   Static Balance   12
   Regaining Balance   15
   Acceleration Away from Balance   17
   Balance While Rotating   19
   Summary   21

3 MOTIONS WITHOUT TURNS   25
   Acceleration from Rest   26
   Motion in a Curved Path   29
   Stopping Horizontal Motion   31
   Vertical Jumps   31
   Combined Vertical and Horizontal Motions   33
   The *Grand Jeté* "Floating" Illusion   34
   The Effect of Turnout on Traveling Jumps   36
   Dance Floors—Elasticity and Friction   39
   Summary   42

4 PIROUETTES   45
   Source of Torque for a *Pirouette*   47
   Controlling Angular Velocity   51
   Characteristics of Different *Pirouettes*   53
   Arabesque Turn   55

Grande Pirouette 59
Fouetté Turns 61
Repeated *Pirouettes* 64
Summary 65

5 TURNS IN THE AIR   69
The *Tour Jeté* 70
The *Demi-fouetté* 73
The *Saut de Basque* 74
The Turning *Assemblé* 77
The *Tour en l'Air* 78
Summary 79

6 EFFECTS OF BODY SIZE   83
Height of a Vertical Jump 84
Entrechats 87
Horizontal Accelerations and Body Size 88
Body Size and *Pirouettes* 89
Adagio Movements 90
Effects of Body Shape 91
Summary 91

7 PARTNERING   95
Vertical Lifts 97
Balance in a Pose 100
A Digression—The Barre as a Partner 104
Supported *Pirouettes*—Balance 106
Supported *Pirouettes*—Control of Rotation 110
Summary 113

8 THE FUTURE   117

APPENDIXES
A LINEAR MECHANICS AND NEWTON'S LAWS   121
B ROTATIONAL MECHANICS   127
C ANATOMICAL DATA FOR A DANCER   132
D MOMENTS OF INERTIA FOR VARIOUS
BODY CONFIGURATIONS   134
E ACCELERATION AWAY FROM BALANCE   138
F OFF-BALANCE *PIROUETTES*   140

G *ARABESQUE* TURN ANALYSIS   142

H QUANTITATIVE ANALYSIS OF THE
   GRANDE PIROUETTE   147

I QUANTITATIVE ANALYSIS OF THE
   FOUETTE TURN   150

J BALANCE IN POSE WITH PARTNER   151

GLOSSARY OF DANCE TERMS USED IN
THIS BOOK   155

GLOSSARY OF PHYSICS TERMS USED IN
THIS BOOK   158

INDEX   161

Foreword

Dancers recognize that they must spend a substantial amount of time keeping their bodies finely tuned to meet the demands of performance. They must also recognize that the mind is engaged just as actively. There is always a search for new insights into dance—ways of expressing ideas, ways of looking at or analyzing movement, or ways of teaching and learning.

This book provides one of those insights. Understanding the physical principles behind human body movement does not mean compromising the aesthetic aspect. It just makes what the body is doing (and what it isn't doing) more understandable. Observers of dance can benefit from these insights through a deepened appreciation of what they see, just as dancers can benefit from a deeper understanding of how their own bodies are working.

Dancers have at least a feeling for the physical processes occurring in dance movement. But we often don't know *why* rapid *pirouettes* or *entrechats* are more difficult for tall dancers than short, or *why* certain characteristics of a *grand jeté* can enhance the "floating" illusion.

The author, although a physicist, is clearly quite familiar with ballet. The way science is applied to dance is valid. (The detailed scientific analyses are there in the appendixes for those who wish that degree of detail.) And people of unquestioned stature in the world of dance—Lisa de Ribère, Sean Lavery, and Martha Swope—have contributed their ideas and support to this project.

Those who have made the most significant contributions to dance—from Bournonville to Balanchine, from Diaghalev to Kirstein—have recognized that developing new perspectives and understandings of dance enriches the art form. The analytical approach represented in this book is one of those new perspectives.

Peter Martins

x

Preface

I am a physicist who "discovered" dance later in life than most people who take it seriously. I began ballet classes long after my way of thinking, based on years of experience in physics, had become well established. This unusual situation has produced a perspective toward dance that is quite different from that of most dancers. As both an observer of dance and a participant in ballet classes and performances, I found my physics background leading to valuable new insights that have given me a deeper appreciation of dance movement. This book describes those insights and approaches I have found so intriguing and useful.

I sincerely believe that *everyone* involved with dance can benefit from the kind of analyses presented in this book. It is true, however, that those who are not used to thinking analytically about an aesthetic art must be willing to accept a challenge—the challenge to expand the horizons of their view of human movement. Open the mind; the rewards can be enormous!

This book is more for the dancer than for the physicist. Dancers will find solutions to some typical problems in specific dance movements, but, more important, should find the *approach* to problems and the resulting basic understanding valuable. Dance teachers will find ways of describing, explaining, or demonstrating dance movement that will add a new dimension to the teaching process. Kinesiologists, dance therapists, and others in dance-related fields should find the information widely applicable. And, of course, those who want to observe dance with a deeper understanding should find a number of interesting ideas here.

Physicists, however, are not excluded. The book includes many examples of applications of physics to the world of easily observable phenomena, and thus has obvious pedagogical value in the teaching of physics. Students of physics often crave practical examples that can be readily observed or, better yet, performed.

The dance movements that make up the subject matter for analysis in this book come from my experience with the Central Pennsylvania Youth Ballet, a dance school and performing company with unusually high standards, and an outstanding level of success with its alumni. (At this time graduates of the school include four members of the New York City Ballet, two members of American Ballet Theatre, and many other members of professional companies.) I have been fortunate to gain acceptance as a rare "non-youth" in the Youth Ballet, and owe an enormous debt of gratitude to the Artistic Director, Marcia Dale Weary, and others at the school who have, with remarkable patience, accommodated the unique needs of an older dancer.

Many persons have helped me deal with the challenge of writing science for a non-science audience. One of these stands out for her support, her painstaking comments on the manuscript at all stages of its development, and her patient explanations of many concepts familiar to dancers more experienced than I. This book would have been considerably less without the help of Hannah Wiley, of the Five-College Dance Department in Massachusetts.

I must also express my gratitude to Dickinson College, which supported this project by providing modest funds and an environment conducive to its completion.

THE ARTISTS

Two dancers who received early training at the Central Pennsylvania Youth Ballet served as models for the photographs in this book—Lisa de Ribère and Sean Lavery.

Lisa is a native of York, Pennsylvania; she received early training also at the school of the Pennsylvania Ballet. After three years at the School of American Ballet she joined Balanchine's New York City Ballet at the age of 16.

CHAPTER 1

Introduction

THE ROLE OF PHYSICAL ANALYSIS

Most dance enthusiasts—dancers, teachers, and spectators—consider dance to be a purely aesthetic performing art, involving human body movement performed to music. They recognize that the challenge for the dancer is to communicate to an audience the visual images intended by the choreographer and the dancer. Many also realize that part of the enjoyment of dance depends on recognizing the difficulty of performing these movements well, making physically challenging steps appear smooth and graceful. Few, however, take the further step of analyzing movements physically in order to *understand* the difficulties facing the performer. Why are certain movements particularly difficult? Which movements are illusions that appear to violate fundamental physical principles? How does a dancer create these illusions? How do dancers use physical principles of motion to their advantage, rather than fight against them?

For example, no matter how much a dancer may wish to leap off the floor and *then* start turning (for a *tour jeté*, for instance—a turning leap) the law of conservation of angular momentum absolutely prevents such a movement. But an understanding of the basic physical principles underlying that movement allows the dancer to create an effective *illusion* of jumping into the air and then turning.

There is a legitimate fear that the aesthetic impact of dance may be sacrificed if one tries to analyze the art form scientifically. A newspaper dance critic reporting on a scientific study of *pirouettes* headed his article, "He Wants

Figure 1-1. Gelsey Kirkland and Mikhail Baryshnikov in "Other Dances." (Photo © 1983 Martha Swope)

to Reduce Ballet to a Science."[1] (The obvious bias was not shared by the investigator!)

The reduction of dance to a science ignores the aesthetic dimension and the essence of communication with an audience. As philosopher Suzanne Langer put it:

In watching a dance, you do not see what is physically before you—people running around or twisting their bodies; what you see is a display of interacting forces. . . . But these forces . . . are not the physical forces of the dancer's muscles. . . . The forces we seem to perceive most directly and convincingly are created for our perception; and they exist only for it.[2]

There's also a feeling that science doesn't really apply to aesthetic art forms. Bart Cook, a member of the New York City Ballet, was quoted a few years ago in a *Dance Magazine* interview as saying, "It's that vision of freedom you create when you're defying physical law. . . ."[3] And Lisa de Ribère, a soloist with American Ballet Theatre, who has submitted her talents to scientific scrutiny, has said that an understanding of physical principles is useful to a dancer in developing technique, but the last thing she would want to think about when on stage in front of an audience is controlling her moment of inertia or maximizing an angular momentum in a turn! Artistic sensitivities *must* occupy one's full attention at that time.

Since a focus exclusively on physical analysis may detract from performance or appreciation of dance as an art form, what is the value of such analysis? Dancers, dance teachers, and people in the medical professions are now recognizing the importance of a knowledge of anatomy for allowing dancers to use their bodies most effectively and safely. A knowledge of anatomical limitations and constraints on human body movement can help prevent the kinds of injuries that interrupt many promising dance careers. And understanding how the muscles work in dance movement, what constraints are imposed by muscles

[1]Daniel Webster, *Philadelphia Inquirer,* April 4, 1978.
[2]Suzanne K. Langer, "The Dynamic Image: Some Philosophical Reflections on Dance," in *Problems of Art* (New York: Scribners, 1957), p. 5.
[3]*Dancemagazine,* September, 1978.

and bones, and how much a young dance student can expand the range of motion permitted by these constraints is clearly a valuable tool for a dance teacher. An example is a *grand battement devant*, in which the structure of the hip prevents maintaining a complete turnout through the upper range of the motion. The good teacher knows and teaches the ideal positions and body configurations, but recognizes the distinction between the ideal and the possible. Teaching involves a balance between eliciting the best possible technique from dancers and recognizing human limits.

But analyzing dance can contribute still more fundamentally to the skill a dancer uses in creating this art. Although dancers cannot see themselves totally in physical terms, as massive bodies moving through space under the influence of well-known forces and obeying physical laws, neither can they afford to ignore these aspects of movement. According to Allegra Fuller Snyder, former head of the Dance Department at UCLA:

Dance is more than an art. It is one of the most powerful tools for fusing the split between the two functions of the brain—the fusing of the logical with the intuitive, the fusing of the analytical perceptions with the sensorial perceptions, the fusing of holistic understanding with step by step thinking. It is a discipline which within itself deals with basic understanding of human experience, and conceptualization.[4]

The science of physics deals with the motion and interaction of material bodies. Its development over the centuries has given rise to laws of motion that are always observed to be valid with a high degree of accuracy. With careful analyses these laws can be applied to dance movement with results that are intriguing, instructive, useful, and at times surprising. The resulting understanding, if used with a proper perspective, can *contribute* to an appreciation of the art form, not detract from it. The aim in this book is not only to create a collection of analyzed movements, but to articulate the techniques of analysis so that the reader can extend these techniques to other

[4]Allegra Fuller Snyder, unpublished address to the Faculty, Department of Dance, University of California at Los Angeles, fall, 1974.

instances in the infinite variety of body movements observed in dance.

PHYSICS AND DANCE

How is the role of physics in dance best illustrated? Mathematical equations are useful only when insight into the applicable physical principles is already established. Thus most of the material in this book deals with descriptions and illustrations of applications of physical laws and concepts. Some of the more detailed or quantitative discussions appear in the appendixes.

Dance consists of both movement and line or position; it has both dynamic and static aspects. Most of the applications of physics have to do with the response of the body to the forces that lead to *movement*. To which aspect is the *aesthetic* quality attributable? The eye clearly sees both instantaneous line or position *and* movement, but are they both perceived simultaneously, or does the mind emphasize one or the other at a particular time?

There is a principle of physics, called the "Principle of Complementarity," which applies to observations of small particles or waves. According to that principle one can see the wave-like properties (movement) of an entity clearly if one sacrifices seeing at the same time the particle-like aspects (position). Similarly one can accurately measure an entity's position if its state of motion is not simultaneously measured with comparable accuracy. Perhaps the eye and mind have a similar "complementarity" when human body motion is observed!

Good dance photography involves a subtle challenge to portray movement with static visual displays. The challenge is particularly crucial when the purpose of the photography is to illustrate the applicability of physical principles that apply mostly to movement. The transitions and accelerations from one configuration to the next are particularly amenable to physical analysis, and are particularly fruitful in contributing to an understanding of dance movement. But how does one illustrate these transitions visually? Is it possible to portray a transitory moment without destroying the aesthetic sense of the position as belonging to dance? An example is a *tombé* movement, which is discussed in chapter 3 (and illustrated in figures 2-6 and 3-4) as it contributes to a horizontal acceleration away from a balance condition. A still photograph of the movement in progress shows the lean of the body that is related to the acceleration, but does it look like dance? The viewer has to imagine the motion associated with the position in order to grasp the full significance of the illustration.

The photographs and diagrams in this book must be accepted with their intent in mind. The dancers are sometimes called upon to demonstrate a particularly important instant in a movement, which may not be the moment one is used to seeing in a dance photograph, or even seeing in the mind's eye during the performance of the movement. But these instants do exist in the flow of dance, and are important to contemplate when dance is analyzed physically.

The emphasis in this book is almost entirely on movements of *classical ballet*, not because of a judgment as to the inherent value or worth of that style of dance, but because of the relatively well-defined and accepted "vocabulary" of movements and positions. Although there are variations in the style with which balletic movements are carried out by different dancers working from different choreographers, there is fundamentally a "correct" way of performing a *tour jeté*, a *pirouette en dehors*, or a *cabriole en avant*. Analyses of these movements therefore have a generalizable applicability that is potentially useful for any dancer performing dance movements.

Modern dance, jazz dance, and even some forms of folk dance share with ballet many similarities in the types of movements on which these styles are based. Turns on one foot are turns whether executed in balletic form with the gesture leg in a *retiré* position or with some other body position called for by the style of the dance. Jumps, leaps, partnered lifts, balance positions, and essentially any other type of dance movement one can imagine can all be analyzed using the techniques described in the following chapters. Ballet is merely the most convenient vehicle for the analyses since it is the most well-defined, constant, and universal style of dance.

One of the challenges in dealing with technical aspects

of dance involves the use of appropriate vocabulary and terminology. How is a basis for communication established between such disparate fields as physics and dance? One characteristic of science is that it is built on precise definitions of pertinent terms. These definitions are intended to be as objective as possible so that they are universally usable, independent of the unique interpretations of individuals. Physicists may disagree on interpretations of observations, but they depend on an assumed agreement concerning the definitions of the terms.

People dealing with dance depend on language to serve two functions. One is to be a vehicle for communicating ideas from one person to another. The second is to form meaningful images in terms of dancers' individual senses of body and movement. A dance teacher may communicate words that have objective definitions, but unless students can translate those words into images in their own bodies, the information transfer is abstract and not useful.

Individual students, because of different ages and backgrounds, have different levels and kinds of understanding. Dance teachers, who often deal with young people lacking a sophisticated vocabulary, create images that seem to work, building on common understandings of how it "feels" to perform certain movements or maintain certain body positions. "Feel as if your body is squeezed into a drinking straw" may communicate successfully the physical idea "Maintain a compact alignment around a vertical axis in order to perform a controlled turn." Or, more physical yet, "Minimize your moment of inertia around a vertical axis so that the torque and angular momentum needed for a given rate of turn will be miminized." The message is the same; the frame of reference is determined by the student's background and intellectual capacity. (The physical principles applicable to this movement—the *pirouette*—are discussed in chapter 4 and appendixes A and B.)

When learning or improving a particular movement, a dancer usually depends on three methods: trial and error as adjustments are made in the basic motions, the example of an experienced dancer executing the motion correctly, and instructions from a teacher or peer. The instructions are often based on an idea of what makes the movement "right."

Although the validity of these traditional methods of learning has been well proven historically, improved techniques for teaching dance are becoming available. An additional basis for learning is a more analytical understanding of how a particular body position or change in body configuration contributes to the desired form.

The example described above, involving placement for a *pirouette*, may be extended. An instructor may tell a student to stretch vertically, pushing into the floor with the supporting foot while reaching for the ceiling with the head. The student finds that a strong and straight vertical body makes the *pirouettes* more successful. And the student observes dancers with weak or flaccid backs having trouble with *pirouettes*. An analysis shows why these aspects of body placement contribute to successful *pirouettes*. If the body is properly "pulled up," the mass is compacted close to the axis of rotation, decreasing the moment of inertia (see appendix B) and allowing for a substantial rate of turn. Such placement is thus not only desirable for aesthetic reasons, but also necessary in order to achieve a reasonable turn rate.

Although difficult physical feats are often accomplished by pure strength and agility, it is sometimes true that the appearance of performing certain movements is illusory, and a deeper skill is required of the dancer in creating these illusions. For the dancer or dance teacher, the understanding resulting from a physical analysis of movement provides a basis for developing techniques for creating or enhancing the illusion of performing the impossible.

It is also true that an *observer* watching a dance performance can appreciate dance movement more deeply with an understanding both of the limitations imposed by physical law and of the role of illusion. Dance movement often inspires awe in the observer, not only because of the beauty of the moving human form, but also because the dancer seems to defy normal physical constraints nature imposes on moving objects. An understanding of the appropriate physical principles allows the spectator to distinguish between possible and impossible movements, and to appreciate the subtle skill of a dancer who creates an illusion of performing the impossible.

What physical principles are pertinent to an analysis of dance? Newton's laws of motion form the basis of any analysis of motions of massive objects. Conservation of linear and angular momentum and the relationship between forces or torques and the resulting changes in the state of motion are principles derived from Newton's laws. (See appendixes A and B.) These principles and laws are deceptively simple to state but enormously powerful when they are carefully applied. Such simplicity and power are sources of awesome beauty in a science such as physics.

Dance movement can be broken down into categories that involve characteristic techniques of analysis. Some movements involve primarily vertical or horizontal motions of the body as a whole, in which rotations can be ignored. These motions can be studied using simple equations of linear motion in three dimensions. The resulting analysis leads to a recognition and understanding of some interesting illusions and techniques, such as the appearance of floating horizontally in a *grand jeté*. Rotational motions require different approaches, involving the way the body's mass is distributed, different axes of rotation for different types of movement, and sources of forces and torques which produce the rotational motion. The simplest rotational motions are *pirouettes* of all types, but there are other movements that involve rotations around horizontal axes (*entrechats*) or skewed axes (*tours jetés*). These will be discussed in later chapters.

Physical analyses can make important contributions to an understanding of the effects of the size of dancers on the movements they can perform. Most choreographers and teachers recognize that small dancers do have different ways of moving than taller ones, but just what are the differences? How can teachers avoid expecting the impossible of tall dancers, or choreographers maximize the effectiveness of their use of different sizes of performers? Are there physical principles that make the slender, long-legged "Balanchine" dancers particularly appropriate for Balanchine choreography? Is there a way to choreograph specifically for the talented but "undersized" dancers who can outperform their taller counterparts in particular movements and tempos? Physical analyses can answer many of these questions.

Certainly ballet cannot be "reduced to a science." But the world of dance is large and complex, with many windows through which one can both perceive and illuminate. Through these windows one may see portrayals of characters or images of a culture, spectacular athleticism or lyrical grace, painful years of dancers' discipline, or free expression of human creativity. It is hoped that the view through the window of physical analysis will enhance, not detract from, an appreciation of this art form, and also that it will contribute to the advancement of the art and skill of dance.

CHAPTER 2

Balance

Dance consists of movements of the body interspersed with motionless poses. Often these poses demonstrate balance of the body over a small area of support on the floor. Some of the more breathtaking moments in a ballet occur when a dancer enters a pose, sometimes directly from a moving step, and holds the position while balanced on *pointe* for several heart-stopping seconds. A *pirouette* ending in a motionless balanced pose is particularly impressive. Questions involving balance provide some particularly interesting, often misunderstood, sometimes surprising, but certainly useful applications of physical analysis.

Suppose that one of the dancers serving as models for the movements described in this book, Lisa de Ribère, moves through a choreographed sequence of movements and poses. In the sequence described below there are several occasions where situations involving balance are encountered. We will look at some of the physical principles important in dealing with problems of balance, and look at how an understanding of these principles can help a dancer improve the performance of these movements. And, as will be the case throughout this book, the analyses described, although here applied to classical ballet movements, can be applied to similar forms of movement in other styles of dance.

Lisa's entrance is followed by a simple *arabesque* on *pointe*, held for several beats of the music. She then moves her extended leg down and forward into a *tombé* to the front and begins a *pas de bourrée* moving forwards. The brief sequence ends with a *pirouette en dehors*.

Fig. 2-1. Kyra Nichols in the New York City Ballet production of "The Nutcracker." (Photo © 1983 Martha Swope)

The first balanced *arabesque* on *pointe* is certainly not "simple." Realizing that perfect balance over a small area of support is unlikely, are there subtle movements of the body that will allow her to maintain her balance? If she *is* balanced in *arabesque*, how can she quickly destroy that balance in order to accelerate forwards? Then there is the *pirouette*. If achieving balance in a motionless pose is difficult, isn't it *more* difficult to maintain balance while turning?

Pirouettes, defined as turns in place on one supporting foot, comprise one of the most important forms of movement in dance. The characteristics of rotational motion—angular momentum, forces and torques that produce angular motion, and the effects of the distribution of body mass—are described in chapter 4. The problem of *balance* in a *pirouette* will be dealt with in this chapter since it can be shown that the more complicated effects of rotation can be ignored.

STATIC BALANCE

Our task in analyzing these situations must begin with an understanding of the meaning of balance. Physically, a condition of balance exists if the dancer remains motionless above the area of support and does not fall. The area of support may be quite small in the case of a dancer on *pointe* on one supporting foot, or may be quite large if both feet are flat on the floor and separated, or, as is more common in modern dance, other parts of the body are on the floor. If there is no contact with a partner or other "object," then the floor and gravity are the only sources of forces acting on the dancer's body. (The situation of balance at the barre will be dealt with in chapter 7, on partnering, where the appropriate tools of analysis are developed.) With only the floor for support, the balance condition will be achieved if and only if the center of gravity lies on a vertical line passing through the area of support at the floor. In all cases we will be dealing with, that support area involves the foot or feet.

If the dancer is motionless, the sum of all the forces and torques acting on the body must be zero (see appendix A). Since the only source of a horizontal force is the floor, there will be no horizontal forces at the floor acting on a

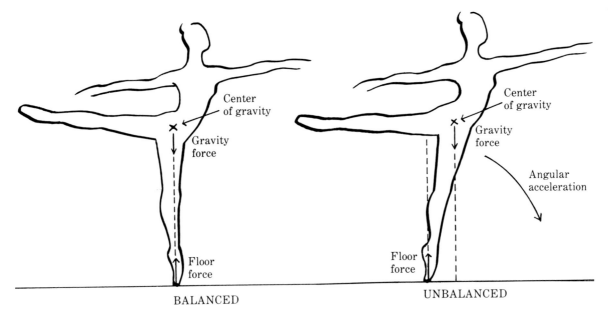

Figure 2-2. Source of torque causing toppling from balance.

motionless, balanced dancer. The force of gravity vertically downward will be balanced by the force upward from the floor to the foot, acting along the same vertical line. If the center of gravity (the location in the body where the mass of the body may be considered to be concentrated) is displaced from the vertical line through the area of support there will result a force couple (see appendix B) which will produce an angular acceleration about a horizontal axis, leading to toppling. Figure 2-2 shows the toppling acceleration resulting from an unbalanced condition.

Clearly, substantial skill is necessary if a dancer is to assume a pose and be balanced over a small area of support. If the pose is entered from a previous horizontal movement such as a run or *chassé*, the center of gravity must coast to a stop just as it reaches that small range of position directly above the support area—less than a square inch for a dancer on *pointe*. Once the center of gravity is within that range of position the foot can be manipulated in such a way that the center of vertical force between the foot and the floor is directly under the center of gravity. When one balances on a flat foot, one can feel the foot moving in such a way as to make small corrections in the center of force within the area of support, thereby maintaining the center of support under the center of gravity, as shown in figure 2-3. In fact, by shifting that center of force, small displacements of the center of gravity may be achieved. It is true, however, that a dancer on *pointe* has such a small area of contact with the floor that it is more difficult to shift the center of force. The only way to accomplish that shift is to move the ankle in a way that shifts the whole area of support horizontally to the desired location. (See figure 2-4). Careful observation shows that any dancer in balance on *pointe* does move the ankle in a small "wavering" motion that represents the necessary movements that maintain balance. The difficulty of the required manipulation is one reason dancing on *pointe* requires strong feet and ankles and much skill!

Actually, a dancer seldom achieves a true balance condition. Suppose the condition of balance is not quite met. If the center of gravity is close to that "balance area," the acceleration away from the vertical is initially quite small. In other words, the closer a dancer is to a perfect balance, the slower will be the fall away from balance. If there is a small initial angle by which the line from the support to the center of gravity is displaced from the vertical, that angle will increase away from the vertical at an accelerating rate.

Figure 2-3.
Shifting the center of supporting force at the floor in order to control balance.

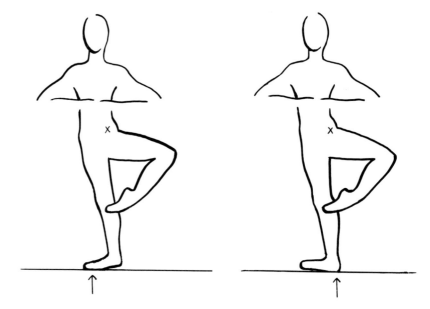

acceleration of the body. (The process of accelerating away from a static position will be discussed in more detail in chapter 3.)

BALANCE WHILE ROTATING

An interesting situation arises when the dancer performs her *pirouette* while trying to maintain balance. Is it possible for an unbalanced, *rotating* dancer to make the subtle corrections necessary to return to a balanced condition?

The first question is whether the toppling motion and correcting body manipulations that maintain balance can be separated from the rotational motion—or whether there would result some complicated motion of the kind observed when a spinning top wobbles off balance (called "precession" in physics). The analysis described in appendix F shows that the rotational motion *can* be ignored when considering balance in normal *pirouettes*.

The problem for the rotating, unbalanced dancer is to try to shift the body position in a subtle way so as to accomplish the same adjustment when rotating that was described before for the *arabesque*, a non-rotating situation. The task is made much more difficult by the rotation, because the direction of adjustment relative to the body must change as the body turns! For instance, suppose the body is off balance, leaning towards stage right while turning to the right. The body must adjust its position in such a way that the floor will exert a horizontal force on the body towards stage left in order to shift the center of gravity back to the vertical line over the area of support. But stage left, the direction the body must move to regain balance, is to the dancer's left when she is facing front, to her rear when she is facing stage right, to her right when she is facing upstage, and so on. The necessary body adjustments are illustrated by Lisa in the poses shown in figure 2-7. Is it possible for a dancer to make these adjustments that must change direction relative to the body as the turn occurs? That is a lot to expect when a turn involves a rotation of perhaps two or three revolutions per second! But if such an adjustment is *not* possible, then the dancer must begin the turn sufficiently close to balance that such adjustments are unnecessary. That also is a lot to expect of a dancer! Again,

a relaxed upper body is necessary to allow for the subtle body adjustments, but a strong lower body provides the support that prevents unwanted wavering.

How is it possible, then, for some dancers to accomplish a multiple *pirouette* of a dozen or so turns without falling? The answer probably involves a combination of several factors. First, the dancer does have to be close enough to balance that at least the first few turns can be accomplished with no adjustment. These turns may indeed be rapid enough that there is some stabilizing effect, as with a spinning top that remains upright because it is spinning. (Such a rapid turn with a rigid body is performed by an ice skater doing very rapid *pirouettes*.) But as the turns become slower because of friction, one can look for those shifts of body position that do change direction as the body turns. This can be observed in a dancer skilled at *pirouettes*, who is asked to try to maintain a turn even when falling out of it. The extreme body adjustments in turns that are significantly off balance can be observed to rotate as the body rotates. It is true that such adjusting motions must occur so rapidly that they may be impossible to teach, meaning that certain people who are "natural" turners have, or can feel and develop, the proper instincts, and others must depend on initially accurate balance in order to accomplish the more usual two- or three-turn *pirouettes*.

SUMMARY

The fundamental techniques used here for analyzing situations involving balance can be applied to an infinite variety of positions. The sources of forces and torques must be identified; then the action of the body that will cause the required forces to be exerted must be found.

For the situations described in this chapter, there are a number of ways dancers and dance teachers can think about solutions to the problems. First, in achieving a

Figure 2-7. The body's reaction to an off-balance *pirouette* must rotate relative to the body as the body rotates. These four posed views, although exaggerated, show the directions of body adjustments that must be made to correct balance in a *pirouette* off balance to the left of the picture.

condition of balance, the center of gravity of the body must be on a vertical line that passes within the area of support. In an *arabesque penché*, for instance, in which the mass of the body shifts forward as the leg rises and the torso leans forward, there must be a conscious effort to allow the body as a whole to shift to the rear so that its center remains over the supporting foot.

When the condition of balance is not quite met, the body can carry out adjusting motions so as to regain balance. These adjustments require either a shift in the center of supporting force at the floor, or a push horizontally against the floor in such a direction as to cause the body to return to the balance configuration. The former is accomplished by adjustments in the supporting ankle or foot; the latter is accomplished by shifting the upper body *towards* the direction of fall. Relaxation of the upper body can contribute to a sensitivity to slight displacements from balance, and make the small subtle adjustments smoother.

Horizontal acceleration away from balance is achieved either by shifting the center of supporting force (by lifting the lead foot, for example) or by a *tombé* or other movement that results in a horizontal force against the floor. Again, the horizontal force against the floor is the important factor.

Balancing while rotating is made difficult by the fact that the direction of adjustment necessary to regain lost balance must shift relative to the body if it is to have the desired direction fixed relative to the world. That is, if the body is tending to fall towards stage right, the direction of adjustments in body position must remain such as to restore the body towards stage left even while the body is rotating relative to the stage. Again, a relaxed upper body will allow these adjustments to remain fluid enough to shift in direction.

The series of *arabesque penchés* on a sloping ramp in *La Bayadère*, a long-held *arabesque* pose on *pointe* in the Sugar Plum Fairy's *pas de deux* from the *Nutcracker*, or Giselle's shifting *attitude* position while hopping on *pointe* along a diagonal, all have similar requirements in terms of balance that can be understood using these principles. The same principles apply to the infinite variety of balanced poses seen in modern dance. And of course Lisa's brief sequence of movements described at the beginning of the chapter is improved as these analyses are applied, up to the point that the movements become automatic, allowing her to occupy her mind with dancing rather than with analysis!

CHAPTER 3

Motions without Turns

Suppose Sean Lavery, our model for the movements to be discussed in this chapter, performs a sequence of jumping and leaping movements. He begins standing upstage left waiting to leap into a series of turning *coupés jetés* around the stage, which pass his partner waiting downstage right. These end in the upper right corner of the stage, where he executes a series of *entrechats six* jumps. A *glissade* and *grand jeté* carry him back towards stage left, where the brief sequence ends.

A number of aspects of this sequence of movements can be understood and some of the problems alleviated with the help of a physical analysis. How does a dancer accelerate quickly away from a standing position? How does he control the forces that produce the acceleration? How does Sean keep himself traveling in a curved path around the stage without colliding with his partner? What must he do to stop quickly when upstage, to avoid coasting into the backdrop? He then must do a series of *entrechats six* jumps, achieving good height with pointed feet in the air while keeping up with the quick tempo; what is the nature of the connection between height of a jump and time in the air? Why does the *grand jeté* seem to be higher than the vertical jumps, and allow for a floating illusion near the peak of the leap? Why does sacrificing turnout seem to contribute to achieving a strong jump? How does he accomplish a landing that is gentle enough to avoid injury, and does not result in slipping and falling? In what way is rosin useful in preventing slipping?

Figure 3-1. American Ballet Theatre's production of "Configurations," with Mikhail Baryshnikov (far left). (Photo © 1983 Martha Swope)

ACCELERATION FROM REST

First let us consider how a dancer can begin a movement from rest, which must involve a quick acceleration away from a standing position. As we found in the chapter on balance, if the body's center of gravity lies on a vertical line above the area of support, and there are no horizontal forces acting on the body, it will be in equilibrium and will remain at rest. If there *is* a net force, an acceleration of the body will occur that is proportional to the force and in the same direction as the force.

Now how does a person arrange to have a force exerted on himself in order to accelerate? For every force exerted by a body against something, the body experiences an equal and opposite force acting back on itself. (This is the third of a powerful set of laws of motion developed by Isaac Newton in the seventeenth century, described in more detail in appendix A.) Since the floor is the only source of a force accessible to the dancer, he must arrange to push against the floor in order to accelerate. If he is initially balanced, it is not easy to exert that horizontal force. In fact, it may take too much time to develop sufficient acceleration to move into the rapid *coupés jetés* described earlier, and yet remain with the music.

What does our dancer do to exert that force against the floor? One mechanism is to *shift the center of force between the feet and the floor.* The center of force may be defined as the point where a distributed force, or several separate forces, may be considered to act. That is, if one's weight is distributed evenly over the supporting foot which is flat on the floor, the center of force is in the center of the foot. Leaning forward so that the weight is forward on the balls of the feet shifts the center of force towards the front of the foot. If the weight is distributed evenly between *two* feet, the center of force is halfway between the feet; if more of the weight is borne by the front foot, the center of force shifts towards the front foot.

Now suppose one wishes to accelerate forward from a standing position. If the feet are spread apart to the front and back, as in a lunge or a wide fourth position, merely lifting the front foot will shift the effective center of force to the rear. (See the diagrams in figure 3-2.) The center of

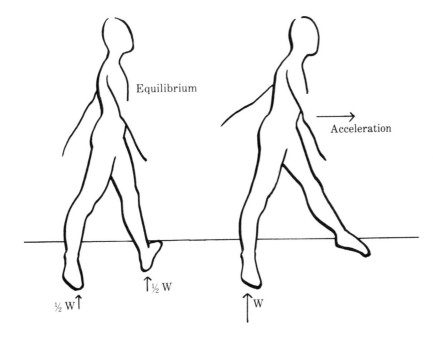

Equilibrium

Acceleration

½ W

½ W

W

Figure 3-2.
Shifting location of
supporting force from two
feet to one foot, producing a
horizontal acceleration.

gravity is then in front of the support, and a fall to the front begins. The back foot can then exert a backwards push against the floor resulting in an acceleration forward.

If the feet are together at the beginning of the movement, the acceleration takes longer, since the center of force cannot be shifted as far horizontally. If the center of gravity is over the balls of the feet, and then the fronts of the feet are lifted, a forward acceleration will result, as shown in figure 3-3.

When the weight of the body is forward on the feet (towards the ball of the foot), one can lift the front of the feet slightly so as to shift the center of force against the floor towards the heel. The center of gravity is then in front of the support as before, and the acceleration can begin. As soon as the center of gravity accelerates to the front, the weight can shift more to the balls of the feet as the body begins walking or running motions.

A familiar example of this mechanism for acceleration is the starting position for a sprinter. Much of the runner's weight is forward on his hands, so that when the hands are lifted, the center of gravity is far forward of his supporting feet, and a large horizontal accelerating force can be

Figure 3-3.
Shifting center of supporting force, destroying balance and allowing for a horizontal acceleration.

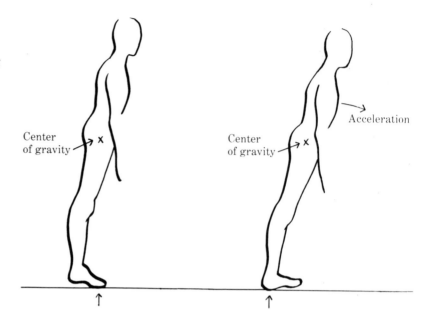

Center of gravity → x

Center of gravity → x

Acceleration

exerted by the feet without their running out from under the rest of the body.

The second mechanism for accelerating from rest involves *thrusting one leg front*, as in a *dégagé* movement often seen at the beginning of a moving combination, and illustrated by Sean in figure 3-4. This movement causes the other (back) foot to push backwards against the floor, resulting in a frontward accelerating force exerted by the floor on the body. This mechanism can exist only for the short time that one part of the body (the gesture leg in this case) is *accelerating* relative to the rest of the body. It is therefore less effective, and is usually used along with the "shifting center of force" mechanism for causing horizontal accelerations.

Our motionless dancer, then, in order to accelerate rapidly with the first beat of the music, must quickly exert a backward force against the floor. He should have his weight forward on his toes, or, better yet, have one foot well in front of the other. Lifting the front foot will allow for a fast acceleration from his initial position. The movement will be more effective if he also swings the front leg frontwards as he begins his acceleration.

Figure 3-4.
Sean Lavery performing a
tombé, or lunge, that allows
for a horizontal acceleration.

MOTION IN A CURVED PATH

Technically, the term "acceleration" refers to any change in velocity, whether an increase or a decrease in speed *or* a change in the direction of motion. Any of these accelerations require an appropriate force. One such horizontal acceleration involves motion in a circular path. That motion may be the *coupés jetés* performed by Sean in the choreography described earlier, or merely running around a stage. Racing tracks are banked at the curves so as to allow the appropriate horizontal accelerating force to be exerted without skidding.

As we have seen, in order for a dancer to achieve a horizontal acceleration, the center of gravity must be displaced from the vertical line over the center of support at the floor, so that the floor can exert a horizontal force. As Sean travels around the stage in his circular path (*manège*), there must be a force on him from the floor directed towards the center of the circle. That force will cause the constant change in his direction of motion that is needed for the curved path. Because of his significant velocity, and because the circle diameter is restricted by the stage size, a sizable lean towards the center is often needed to prevent him from moving off the circle "on a tangent," leaving the stage precipitously. Note Sean's lean in figure 3-5, in which

Figure 3-5.
Turning *coupés-jetés* in a curved path, the common *manège*, often seen in men's variations, require a force from the floor toward the center of the curved path. The lean of the body shown in this photo allows for that force, much as the banking of a curved road allows cars to follow the turn without skidding.

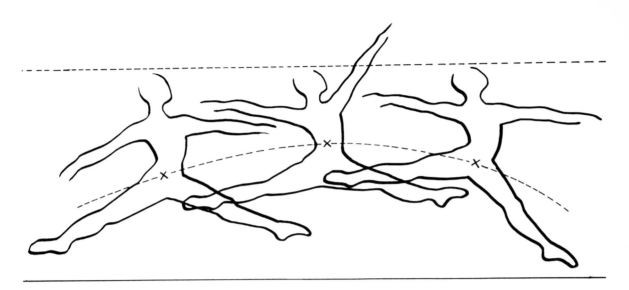

Figure 3-6. The *grand jeté* "floating" illusion, in which the center of gravity follows a parabolic trajectory, but moves its position in the body as the configuration of the body changes.

Although the center of gravity follows a curved trajectory that is determined by the conditions of the initial jump from the floor, the position of the center of gravity *relative to the body* can be moved. Suppose the center of gravity when the dancer first leaps is in the abdominal area, when the legs and arms are rather low. Now when the center of gravity has risen part way through its curved trajectory the arms and legs are raised, causing the center of gravity to move up in the body, perhaps to the stomach or above. If the timing is right, the center of gravity will continue to rise to the peak of the curved path, then begin to fall, while the torso and head of the body actually move horizontally. (See diagram in figure 3-6.) Since the eye of the observer is likely to follow the head and torso, an illusion is created that the dancer is actually floating horizontally for a few brief moments! A necessary component of body motion to accomplish this illusion, then, is the raising of the legs, ideally to a "split," at the peak of the leap. Such a split is often seen in an impressive *grand jeté*, but it is now seen not only as an added flair unrelated to the jump itself, but as a component of the motion contributing directly to this illusion of "floating." But the split must be

Figure 3-7.
Sean Lavery's *grand
jeté*, illustrating the
illusion described in the
accompanying analysis and
shown in the diagram in
figure 3-6.

timed to coincide with the peak of the curved path of the body's center of gravity in order to produce the smoothest appearance of horizontal motion. The sequence of four instants in the *grand jeté* demonstrated by Sean in figure 3-7 shows many of these characteristics.

THE EFFECT OF TURNOUT ON TRAVELING JUMPS

Should a traveling jump such as a *grand jeté* be performed with the feet and legs turned out? The accepted aesthetic quality for essentially all *ballet* movements includes turnout. A *grand jeté* to the side, however, represents one movement in which another important quality, the height of the jump, is sacrificed if turnout is maintained. Compromise is clearly necessary, in which a choreographer's judgment determines the quality most important for the immediate purpose.

Consider two extremes. In the first case the *glissade* preceding the *grand jeté* is performed *en face*, moving directly to the left, with complete turnout, so that the right foot is pointed directly right as the push-off for the *grand jeté* to the left occurs. In the other extreme, the body is turned towards the direction of motion and turnout is sacrificed, so that the *glissade* becomes a running step to

the left, with both feet pointed to the left, in the direction of motion (see figure 3-8).

The jump will be significantly stronger and higher in the latter case. The reason involves the angle through which the push-off foot moves in exerting the force that accelerates the body in the leap. If the right foot is turned out, it is already partially extended at the beginning of the rise of the heel off the floor, when the calf muscles begin to extend the foot, resulting in the force through the foot against the floor. As shown in the diagrams in figure 3-8, the angle through which the force can be exerted is thus less than 90°, from an extended position to a fully extended angle. However, when the foot is pointing in the direction of movement, it is flexed to an acute angle with the leg at the beginning of the jump, and thus can ideally extend through a change of more than 90° to the fully extended position. When the force is exerted through a larger angle of travel of the foot, more energy is contributed to the jump. (The two approaches to the *jeté* are demonstrated by Sean in figure 3-9.)

Of course in the dance movement described, one would never observe either extreme discussed here. There is always some degree of compromise. But it is true that the human body has evolved such that our feet generally point in the direction of movement. This body configuration

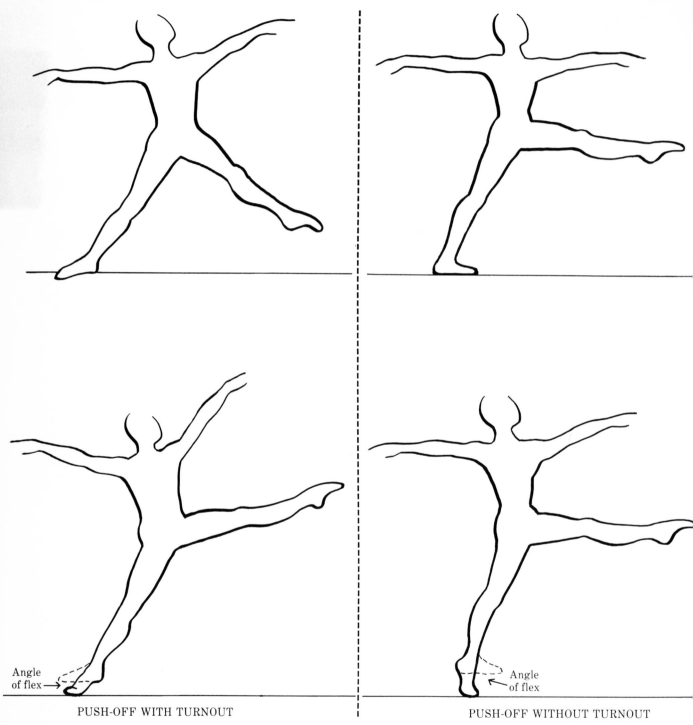

Angle
of flex →

PUSH-OFF WITH TURNOUT

Angle
of flex

PUSH-OFF WITHOUT TURNOUT

Figure 3-8. Push-off for a *grand jeté*, with and without turnout.

contributes to the effective use of the muscles in accomplishing the purpose of running or jumping.

Figure 3-9.
Sean pushing off for a *grand jeté* with and without turnout, as shown in the diagram in figure 3-8.

DANCE FLOORS—ELASTICITY AND FRICTION

The next "event" in this choreography involves the landing from the *grand jeté*. Dancers are well aware of the importance of dance floors for their safety and technique. Both the elastic properties and the surface friction of dance floors are extremely important, and often inadequate for the demands dancers place upon the floors. First let us consider the vertical elastic properties of a floor, which are important for a safe landing. Elasticity involves both large scale "springiness" and small scale "rubberiness." It is commonly recognized that an unyielding floor construction such as concrete is difficult and dangerous to dance on. Does a springy floor aid in the jumping process as a diving board would, or does it allow higher jumps only because of the psychological effect of an anticipated softer landing? Actually the magnitude of vertical motion in a springy floor is rather small—less than an inch—while the vertical displacement of the body's center of gravity during the push-off for a jump is at least a foot. This implies that the contribution of the floor to the magnitude of vertical velocity at the end of the push-off is rather small.

Now let us consider the deceleration, or sudden decrease in downward speed, that occurs as the body lands. Of course the foot will decelerate more rapidly than other parts of the body because it has no other springy part of the body to cushion its fall or extend its deceleration. The torso must decrease its downward velocity from the free fall velocity just before landing to zero, but the bending of the legs allows this velocity change to occur over a sizable distance (perhaps one foot) and an associated time of about one-quarter second. The landing foot and lower leg, however, must lose the same velocity of fall in a much shorter distance. Suppose the sole of a shoe and the padding of flesh between the skin and the bony structure of the foot can compress a total of one-tenth inch. For a jump in which the center of gravity has risen two feet, the downward velocity just before landing is about 11 feet per second. If that velocity changes to zero in a distance of one-tenth inch, the deceleration is about 240 times the acceleration due to gravity, or 240 g! That deceleration can be potentially harmful to the foot. Now if the floor adds additional vertical motion of one inch, the deceleration is only about 10% as great. Thus the seemingly insignificant "give" in the floor results in a large decrease in the potentially dangerous deceleration of the body.

This principle is very evident in some easily observed situations. The air bags used by high jumpers and pole vaulters for their landings extend the time and vertical distance over which the free fall velocity may be decreased to zero. An automobile bumper with some spring to it will cause and sustain less damage than a stiff one. Closer to home, there is less discomfort when one trips and falls if the landing is made on the padded buttocks than on the unpadded head!

Now what benefit is gained from the use of common linoleum or rubber-like stage floors commonly used for dance? The most important properties are probably the controlled uniformity and sound-deadening capability. Many stages have holes, grooves, slippery spots, and other problems that can be covered by a portable dance floor. And the sound of a hard shoe surface (as on the toe of a *pointe* shoe) striking a floor can be decreased substantially by even a small amount of small-scale elasticity. But it is also true that this small-scale "give" in a floor increases the area of contact between the toe of a *pointe* shoe and the floor. On a hard surface the curved toe will ride on the floor with only a very small part of the convex surface making contact. That small part will, of course, have an extremely large pressure due to the body weight, and will wear rapidly. A slightly elastic floor surface will allow the shoe to sink into the surface somewhat, allowing a larger area of contact. Not only should this be easier on the shoe, but the dancer may benefit from a greater "feel" of the floor.

Now we return to the final *grand jeté*, and a dancer's common concern for the potentially slippery floor. Is rosin on the floor always the appropriate solution? What are the principles involved in the frictional properties of floors?

Friction involves the properties of surfaces, both chemical and mechanical. Both chemical adhesion between surfaces and microscopic roughness contribute to a frictional force that acts in a direction tangential to the interface between the surfaces. For many pairs of interacting surfaces the magnitude of the friction force is proportional to the perpendicular force pressing the two surfaces together. The constant of proportionality is called the coefficient of friction.

Rosin is used on a floor to increase friction. Whether a dancer needs a change in linear horizontal motion or an angular acceleration, the floor must be able to supply the horizontal forces that provide for such accelerations. The perpendicular (vertical) force is equal to the person's weight if there are no vertical accelerations, so the only way to increase friction is to change the nature of the surfaces.

Many dance movements involve sliding on the floor, or rotating on a pivoting supporting foot. Too much friction will prevent these movements, which may include *glissades* and *assemblés* in addition to all types of *pirouettes*. One characteristic of rosin is that it has a large static coefficient of friction and a significantly smaller dynamic coefficient. This means that if the foot is stationary on the floor, a large horizontal frictional force is possible, but if the foot is moving, that force is substantially smaller. That difference is very useful to a dancer, who needs the horizontal force only when the foot is not moving against the floor.

Why don't modern dancers, who perform many of the same sorts of movements as ballet dancers, use rosin? Modern dance is usually performed with bare feet. Since the skin is usually somewhat moist (particularly when the body is exercising), the characteristics of the surfaces in contact are different than when dry. A small amount of moisture makes adjoining surfaces less slippery; too much moisture reverses that effect, since there can now be a film of water between the surfaces. The normal skin moisture is appropriate for the movements of a modern dancer, whereas rosin adds more friction than the bare feet can withstand, giving rise to blisters or worse. Ballet dancers often use water on the floor or the shoes to provide a degree of friction similar to that of moist bare feet.

SUMMARY

A dancer performing linear movements—vertical, horizontal, or a combination—must understand and control the forces exerted against the floor. These forces are responsible for the accelerations, or changes in the state of motion. Horizontal acceleration from rest requires a horizontal force against the floor. This force can arise from a shift in the center of supporting force relative to the center of gravity of the body, or from an acceleration of part of the body that results in a force against the floor.

Motion in a curved path requires an acceleration, in this case because of the change in *direction* of the velocity. That acceleration requires a horizontal force, which can come only from a lean towards the center of curvature, as in a banked curve on a road. The faster the motion, or the tighter the turn, the greater the lean from vertical. Friction against the floor is often the limiting factor in establishing how fast or tight the curved motion can be.

Horizontal motion can be stopped only if there is a horizontal force against the floor in the direction of motion (resulting in a force from the floor on the body in a direction such as to slow the motion to a stop). A landing from a jump would have to be made with the center of gravity *behind* the landing foot in order to allow the body to coast to a stop in a stable position.

Vertical jumps require forces against the floor that must be adjusted to produce the height required and the time in the air determined by the rhythm of the music. The relationship between height and duration is fixed by nature, and is independent of body size. A jump four times the height will have a duration twice as long.

In-flight trajectories, involving combined vertical and horizontal motions, *always* have a parabolic shape for the path of the center of gravity. Nothing a dancer does after take-off from the floor can change the trajectory of the center of gravity. The horizontal component of motion in the trajectory is always a straight line while the body is in the air. The vertical component of motion is identical to a jump in place. The illusion of "floating," or temporarily stopping the downward acceleration at the peak of the jump, is accomplished by shifting the position of the center of gravity in the body, so that the torso and head move only horizontally for a short time while the center of gravity continues its parabolic curved trajectory.

The vertical impulse that can be produced for a jump depends on the range of motion of the foot around the ankle pivot. In some cases that range of motion is limited when turnout is maintained, and the height of a jump is sacrificed.

Both elastic and frictional properties of dance floors are important for dancers, the former for vertical motions, and the latter for horizontal accelerations. Elasticity contributes little to the vertical impulse in a jump, but does allow a softer landing that decreases the potential for injury. Rosin is used to increase friction of the feet against the floor because it tends to be sticky when there is *no* motion, but allows motion more easily once the feet are moving on the floor. Thus *glissades* and *pirouettes* are possible at the same time that the friction allowing for rapid accelerations or decelerations is present.

CHAPTER 4

Pirouettes

Turning movements are common in all forms of dance. One of the most common turns is the *pirouette*, or rotation of the body over one supporting foot on the floor. There are many types and styles of *pirouettes*, from a low turn on bent leg in modern dance to *attitude* or *arabesque* turns, *en dehors* or *en dedans* turns, or the spectacular multiple *fouetté* turns or *grandes pirouettes* often seen in the classical ballet repertoire. The various turns have both common aspects and uniquely different characteristics and problems.

Descriptions of these turns will be useful for the analyses that follow. An *en dedans* turn is any *pirouette* toward the supporting leg (a right turn onto the right supporting leg, for instance). An *en dehors* turn is away from the supporting leg (a right turn supported by the left leg, for instance). The normal *pirouette* position in ballet has the supporting leg straight and almost vertical, and the gesture leg raised to the side with the foot at the knee of the supporting leg (sometimes called a retiré position). An *arabesque* turn is usually a *pirouette en dedans* with the leg extended *derrière* in *arabesque* position. *Attitude* turns can be *en dedans* or *en dehors* (more difficult and less common), *en avant* or *derrière*. A *grande pirouette* is a turn with the leg extended horizontally to the side (*à la seconde*). *Fouetté* turns are repeated *pirouettes en dehors* with the gesture leg extended away from the body during a part of each turn when the dancer is facing the audience.

Now let us return to Lisa's sequence described in chapter 2. Her balanced *arabesque* on the left leg was followed by *tombé pas de bourrée* into fourth position in

Figure 4-1. The New York City Ballet's "Serenade." (Photo © 1983 Martha Swope)

preparation for a *pirouette en dehors* on her left leg. (The condition of balance in the *pirouette* was analyzed in chapter 2.) Lisa must end the *pirouette* with a lunge to fourth position *en avant* followed by an *en dedans arabesque* turn on her right leg. She now brings her extended left leg into *retiré* position, thereby increasing her rate of turn markedly. She then stops the *pirouette en dedans* to the right with a lunge to fourth position with the left leg front, from which she starts a series of *fouetté* turns to the right on the left supporting leg. The sequence ends with a couple of successive *pirouettes* from fifth position, also turning to the right on the left supporting leg.

Any *pirouette* must commence with some form of preparation position followed by a torque exerted against the floor. (A torque is a turning force that produces a rotational acceleration; the concept of torque is explained more fully in appendix B.) Since the floor is the only source of forces or torques other than gravity (when there is no contact with a partner or barre), the torque of the floor against the dancer causes the angular acceleration that produces the dancer's turning motion. So the first question one may ask about Lisa's sequence of turns is, "How is the torque exerted effectively against the floor, resulting in the appropriate turning motion?" Some dancers find that the *pirouette en dehors* is easier when started from a wider fourth position (greater distance between front and back feet) and a straight back leg, as demonstrated by Lisa in figure 4-3. Why is that?

The following *arabesque* turn requires more force from the feet in order to achieve a reasonable turn rate, and still is a slower turn than a *pirouette* in *retiré* position. Why is that? In the process of trying to control the turn rate in an *arabesque* turn, the gesture leg tends to descend during the turn, then rise again. What physical principles govern that oscillating motion, and what can a dancer do to combat it? Is the body configuration for balance different for this rotating condition than for a stationary body in a similar position? Why does the turn rate increase when the gesture leg is brought from the horizontal *arabesque* position to *retiré*, closer to the body?

Fouetté turns, in which the gesture leg is extended during part of each turn, are made easier if the rotation of the body is momentarily stopped during that part of each revolution. But how does the body get rid of the rotational motion suddenly, and then regain it? What is the role of the extended gesture leg? The final successive *pirouettes* from fifth position are also made easier if the body can slow or stop its rotation for a moment in each turn. How is the slowing accomplished in this case?

Let us now analyze each of the movements in this combination, along with the potential problems and some possible solutions. In a preparation position for any turn, the body must be prepared to exert a downward push against the floor that will raise the body's center of gravity for the turn, and to exert horizontal forces with the feet to produce the angular acceleration. The important "placement" that instructors work so hard to achieve in their students allows these forces to be exerted without distortions of the body that prevent the necessary balance, body position, and rate of turn from being achieved. For instance, an incorrect tilt of the pelvis, or "sitting in the hip," may distort the body so that it wobbles around the rotation axis rather than revolving symmetrically.

For most turns, the rotational motion is developed from the torque exerted on the body by the floor, which results from the torque exerted by the body against the floor through the two feet. (The process of exerting the torque with the feet is described in the next section.) Since *pirouettes* are turns *in place*, the *total* horizontal force must be zero to prevent linear acceleration away from the position where the turn is to take place. In fact, the most common reason for a dancer falling out of a *pirouette* is that the *relevé* is not directly upward, the total horizontal force at the beginning of the turn is not zero, and the center of gravity *does* move away from a position of balance above the supporting foot.

SOURCE OF TORQUE FOR A *PIROUETTE*

Since air resistance represents a force small compared to other forces acting on the body, the only significant horizontal forces will be those from the floor acting on the feet. When a dancer exerts a horizontal force against the floor, Newton's third law tells us that the floor exerts an

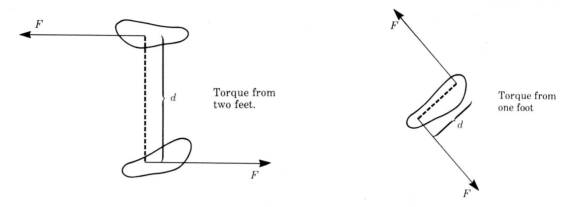

Figure 4-2. Force couples and torques between the feet and the floor, which produce the turning motion for *pirouettes.*

equal and opposite force against the dancer's foot (see appendix A). This then is the source of the external force acting on the body that can produce motion.

No change in *angular* motion of the body can take place unless there is a torque. (See appendix B for the physical basis of the following discussions of angular motion.) For a turn in place, the total horizontal force on the body is zero, and the torque is produced by a force "couple." There must be two equal and opposite forces F exerted by the feet with some distance d between the lines of action of the forces, as shown in figure 4-2. The torque can be made larger by increasing either F or d.

The torque to initiate a turn can be exerted against the floor by two feet with some distance d between them, or by one foot, where the distance d is no greater than the length of the foot. The implications are clear: a turn from fifth position, with a small distance d, requires more force to produce the same torque than a turn from fourth position, in which d is larger. Requiring even more force, and therefore more difficult, is a turn in which the torque is exerted by just the supporting foot while it is still flat on the floor. In the case of a *pirouette en dedans,* for example, the torque exerted by the two feet acting together ends when one foot leaves the floor; the torque from the single supporting foot ends when that foot rises onto *pointe* or *demi-pointe,* at which time the distance d across which a force couple can be exerted becomes very small, and torque

angular momentum, thus slowing the rate of turn of the rest of the body. In order to minimize the effect of the spotting head on the angular velocity of the rest of the body, the head must be kept on the axis of rotation, where its moment of inertia is small.

When the turn is to be stopped, the foot (or feet) return flat to the floor, allowing the retarding friction to increase, and the arms are extended, which slows the angular velocity for the angular momentum remaining. Coordinating these two actions of the body allows the turn to end in the desired orientation.

CHARACTERISTICS OF DIFFERENT *PIROUETTES*

The differences between different types of turns may now be analyzed. The examples will all be from the classical ballet vocabulary, but again the results may be generalized to other forms of turns. Recall the *pirouette en dehors* and *en dedans*, *arabesque* and *attitude* turns, *grandes pirouettes*, and *fouetté* turns described earlier.

Experiments performed by the author have provided some detailed information about the mechanics of these turns.[1] The experiments consisted of measuring the angular momentum of a platform that was free to rotate, on which a dancer performed various types of turns. By conservation of angular momentum, the L of the dancer was equal and opposite to the L of the platform, so that the time-varying total angular momentum of the dancer was determined by merely measuring the rate of turn of the platform. The rate of change of this turn rate is a measure of the torque being exerted. A number of conclusions were reached from these experiments:

1. For a *pirouette en dehors*, all of the torque comes from the two feet exerting forces a distance d apart, where d is the distance between the feet. There is no torque after the gesture foot leaves the floor. This result is reasonable, since it is clearly very difficult to exert a torque in the proper direction with the supporting foot, if that foot is already well turned out in the preparatory position. (That

[1]Kenneth Laws, "An Analysis of Turns in Dance," *Dance Research Journal 11*, 1 & 2, (1978–79).

turnout in preparatory position is part of the "correct" technique for *pirouettes* in classical ballet.) It is also true that if a sizable angular momentum is needed, then it is self-defeating to try to rise onto the supporting foot too rapidly, since that cuts short the amount of time the torque can be applied. It is also important to exert the torque with arms extended, so as to produce a large moment of inertia I, thereby allowing the body to develop angular momentum without too much initial angular velocity. When the arms are brought closer to the body, the angular velocity then increases. It helps to allow the lead arm to begin moving in the direction of the turn before the rest of the body starts turning, in order to acquire some of the necessary angular momentum early in the turn.

2. Turns *en dedans* (*pirouettes* with or without *dégagé à la seconde, attitude* turns, and *arabesque* turns) may be initiated with a substantial part of the torque coming from the supporting foot. The push-off foot leaves the floor early, while the supporting foot is still flat and able to exert the "single-foot torque" described earlier. Since the turn is toward the supporting foot, that foot (and leg) will be turning in as the turn starts. A good dancer will turn it out again quickly when rising onto *pointe* or *demi-pointe*, but there will be a short time when the foot is turned in. For the *pirouette en dedans*, about one-third of the torque comes from the supporting foot alone after the push-off foot has left the floor. In the *arabesque* turn, about 15% of the torque comes from the supporting foot alone.

3. The total length of time from the beginning of the acceleration to the moment the push-off foot leaves the floor is remarkably similar (about one-half second) for the *pirouette en dehors* and the *arabesque* turn, a result that was quite reproducible. The *en dedans* turn with *dégagé à la seconde* had a smaller time (about one-third second) before the push-off foot left the floor, but the supporting-foot torque continued for a few tenths of a second before the maximum angular momentum was attained.

4. The total angular momentum was least for *pirouettes en dehors* and greatest (about 30% larger) for *arabesque* turns. This is interesting in that the rate of turn is faster (more than double) for the *pirouette en dehors* than for the *arabesque* turn. Clearly the moment of inertia

is of crucial importance, being greatest for the *arabesque* turn with extended leg. So even though a greater angular momentum is achieved for such a turn, the angular velocity is small because of the large moment of inertia.

5. "Spotting" the head during the turn is quite different for the two turns. In the *pirouette en dehors* the head turns a full circle in about one-quarter second (the same for the first and the second turn), which is about one-half of the time for the full turn. In the slower *arabesque* turn, the head is turning for a full second, almost 80% of the total time of the turn. In fact, often the head does not spot, but moves with the rest of the body in the slow *arabesque* turn.

6. In all cases there was less total angular momentum on *pointe* than on *demi-pointe*. Apparently the smaller friction from *pointe* shoes allows the dancer to remain turning longer than with soft shoes, so not as much effort is required for the turn. It is also true that the positions require more delicate adjustments on *pointe*, and that large torques would make these adjustments more difficult.

Although these numerical results are reported for experiments with just one dancer, preliminary trials with student dancers showed the same general characteristics. Lisa de Ribère, one of the models for all of the dance movements described in this book, provided her generous assistance and comments in these studies. The results of Lisa's *pirouettes* showed a remarkable consistency in the shape of the angular momentum graph for a particular type of turn, even when some trials were considered better than others in aesthetic form, as evaluated by Lisa herself and dance instructors who viewed the films. Over 50 trials were recorded and analyzed on two different occasions.

ARABESQUE TURN

An *arabesque* turn in classical ballet is a beautiful movement when performed well. Unfortunately, there is a common error one can observe in students learning the movement. The prevalence of this error has an interesting physical reason behind it.

The *arabesque* turn is usually an *"en dedans"* turn, rotating towards the supporting leg. It requires exerting the torque with the two feet on the floor, then lifting the push-off leg into a horizontal position to the rear, where it is not visible to the dancer. After the leg reaches the horizontal position there is a strong tendency for it to drop lower, as in a *grand battement derrière,* or kicking movement to the rear. When the leg is fully extended horizontally, it represents a large contribution to the total moment of inertia of the body, which makes the angular velocity (rate of turn) small for the magnitude of angular momentum that resulted from the initial torque. When the leg drops, its mass is not as far from the axis of rotation, so the moment of inertia is decreased. This reduced moment of inertia allows the angular velocity to increase, making the turn seem easier, faster, and more satisfying. The drooping leg, since it is behind the body, is not easily seen by the dancer (except in a mirror).

An interesting phenomenon now occurs. Since the angular velocity has increased, there is an increased centrifugal force away from the axis of rotation tending to throw the leg out towards the horizontal again! So a dancer may experience an oscillation of the leg up to the horizontal, down, then up again, possibly repeated for a multiple *arabesque* turn (see figure 4-4). In fact, such an oscillation can be observed in students who do not concentrate on keeping the leg fixed in the *arabesque*

Figure 4-4.
"Drooping" leg in an *arabesque* turn.

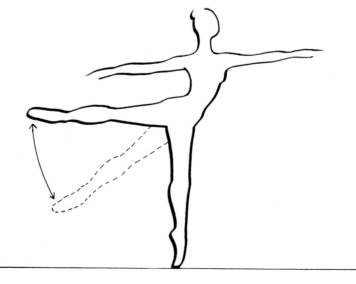

position, as detected by proprioceptive senses—the internal senses the mind uses to determine body positions without visual cues. One may ask if this oscillating leg syndrome is bad; perhaps the choreographer intends such a movement! But the traditional *arabesque* turn in ballet, which is a common and impressive movement, is done ideally with the gesture leg fixed in a horizontal position. Choreographers do sometimes depart from the ideal for artistic reasons, and similar turns in other styles of dance may depart in specific details from the classical ballet model.

Lisa de Ribère performed the arabesque turn with the "drooping leg" for the camera in order to illustrate the problem. Considering the beautiful line she normally maintains in arabesque turns, the difficulties she experienced were mild! The resulting sequence of photographs is shown in figure 4-5.

At what frequency might the gesture leg be oscillating up and down? The problem is not a simple one, because the centrifugal effect tending to throw the leg out depends on the angular velocity of the turning body, but that angular velocity itself depends on the angle the gesture leg makes with the vertical.

It often happens in physics that parts of a problem can be formulated in a straightforward way, but when the parts are interdependent they cannot be solved separately. The combined problem becomes sufficiently complex that it is difficult to solve directly. At this point one can turn to the computer for a numerical solution, which is fruitful if the numerical values of the important parameters are known. In this case it is better to take another approach—that of making as many approximations and guesses as necessary in order to reduce the problem to one that is solvable. The information thus obtained may not be totally accurate, but we must keep in mind that we are looking for generalizable characteristics of movement that will apply to a variety of different body shapes and sizes, positions, rates of turn, and so on.

In this case several approximations were made, beginning with a leg modelled as a straight cylinder uniform in thickness over its length, free to oscillate in a vertical plane from the hip, with the pivot lying on a

Figure 4-5.
Sequence of five consecutive instants in an *arabesque* turn, demonstrating the "drooping" leg problem. The gesture leg oscillates down and up once during the complete turn shown.

vertical line above the point of support (the foot of the vertical supporting leg). As shown in appendix G, the moment of inertia can be found for the gesture leg as a function of the angle the leg makes with the vertical. This moment of inertia then determines the instantaneous angular velocity, which in turn determines the outward centrifugal force, and this, in combination with the effect of gravity on the gesture leg, helps determine the angle the gesture leg makes with the vertical. In order to make the resulting equations solvable, it was assumed that the total angular momentum was such that the leg's equilibrium angle was 45°, and that the oscillations around that angle were small. For a typical length of leg there is a resulting equation which relates the oscillation frequency of the leg to the rotation frequency.

An interesting result is found for a body size and shape typical of dancers, and a typical *arabesque* turn rate. The leg's oscillation frequency is equal to the rotation frequency when the dancer takes about two seconds to complete a full turn. If we keep in mind that there are some crude approximations involved, it does turn out to

be reasonable to expect that for a typical rotation rate for an *arabesque* turn (a full turn every one or two seconds) the leg may oscillate up and down at the same frequency; that is, once each revolution. This resonance between the two frequencies may make it particularly difficult to overcome this oscillating leg problem, since the natural frequency of that oscillation makes it "bounce" just once each revolution! The good *arabesque* position would occur when the body is facing one direction, then occur again when the body returns to that orientation. In between, the dancer rotates rapidly when the leg is lower.

GRANDE PIROUETTE

Another interesting effect occurs in a *grande pirouette*, and also in other turns with a straight extended gesture leg, such as Lisa's *arabesque* turn described earlier. Since the body position for the *grande pirouette* is identical to a stationary pose often seen—the body *en face* with the gesture leg horizontal to the side *à la seconde*—one might wonder if the condition for balance is the same whether

Figure 4-6. Second position *en l'air*, stationary and turning. The condition for balance is slightly different in the two cases, with the supporting leg closer to vertical when the body is rotating.

the body is rotating or not. The physical analysis of the condition for balance for a *static* body is straightforward, involving the masses, lengths, and positions of the various body segments. As shown in the photograph in figure 4-6a, the supporting leg is not quite vertical because of the amount of weight that is extended to one side. For typical body segment masses and lengths, one can calculate the angle the supporting leg makes with the vertical. This angle is about 4½° for a male dancer. (The *grande pirouette* is more often performed in ballet by male dancers.)

Now suppose the body is rotating about a vertical axis through the supporting foot. If the supporting leg again makes an angle of 4½° will the body be in balance while rotating? Strangely enough, no! Because the body position for the *grande pirouette* is not bilaterally symmetric, the angular momentum must precess (as with a spinning top that is wobbling) around the vertical axis. That precession of the angular momentum, necessary for a balanced turn, requires an angle between the supporting leg and the vertical that is less than $4\frac{1}{2}°$; in fact, about $3\frac{1}{2}°$ for the same data used for the static equilibrium. (See appendix H for a more detailed analysis of the *grande pirouette*.) Although this difference in balance angle is small, and variations in the performance of the movements are often large enough to mask the effect, the photographs of Sean in figure 4-6 do seem to show a slight difference in angle.

Although the shift in balance position is small, good dancers must be sensitive to very small shifts in position in order to achieve the remarkable feats of balance sometimes observed. Without a sensitivity to this shift in balance condition when the body is rotating, it is more difficult to carry out the movement well.

FOUETTÉ TURNS

The *fouetté* turn is a repeated *pirouette* that begins as a normal *pirouette en dehors* but includes a movement that allows the angular momentum lost to friction to be regained once each revolution. Properly done *fouetté* turns are an impressive tour de force in a ballerina's vocabulary. One of the best-known examples in standard classical choreography is the 32 continuous *fouetté* turns by the Black Swan in act 3 of "Swan Lake."

This turn is one of the few continuing turns, a fact that suggests the immediate question, "How does the dancer maintain balance and replace angular momentum lost by friction indefinitely?" The turn itself is a series of repeated *pirouettes* with a pause in the turn after each full rotation. While the body is turning it is in a normal *pirouette* position, with the arms forming a circle to the front and the gesture leg to the side with the foot at the knee of the supporting leg. When the body and head are facing front, the gesture leg is extended to the front, the arms start to open, and the supporting leg is bent slightly, in a *plié* with heel down. As the gesture leg moves from front to side it absorbs the angular momentum of the turn while the torso, head, and arms remain facing the audience.

When the gesture leg is brought in to the knee of the supporting leg again, and the dancer rises onto straight leg and pointed foot, the whole body again turns through a complete revolution, since the angular momentum is now shared by the entire rotating body. The period of time during which the dancer's body is not rotating (less than one-half second) provides an opportunity for regaining balance and exerting some torque against the floor with the flat supporting foot, thus regaining any momentum lost by friction.

The sequence of photographs in figure 4-7 shows Lisa in various stages of a *fouetté* turn. Starting at the top, a clockwise path through the six pictures shows the stages of the movement in proper order, and may be continued for the repeated turns.

What characteristics of this movement can be changed by a choreographer or a dancer without destroying the movement itself? What characteristics are dictated by physical principles, and which are determined by aesthetic considerations? An important aspect of the turn is the motion of the gesture leg from front to side while the body is temporarily stationary. In fact, a common error of students learning this movement is to thrust the leg directly to the side, an action which of course slows the rotation because of the increase in moment of inertia, but does not allow the torso, head, and arms to stop briefly. It is also necessary to have the gesture leg extended as far from the rotation axis of the body as possible in order for it to absorb the total angular momentum of the turn without acquiring too large an angular velocity.

Quantitative calculations have been made based on weights and dimensions of body segments for an average female dancer, using an idealized model of body positions for a good *fouetté* turn. Suppose a dancer is doing a normal *pirouette* at a rotation rate of two revolutions per second. When the body is facing front the gesture leg is extended forward and begins rotating to the side while the remainder of the body remains non-rotating. If the total

pirouettes from fifth position involve a more subtle transfer of momentum which is based on the same principle. In this case the angular momentum is transferred to the arms, which temporarily rotate relative to the rest of the body while the dancer is facing front.

CHAPTER 5

Turns in the Air

Our model for the dance movements to be discussed in this chapter is Sean Lavery of the New York City Ballet. His next choreographed sequence starts downstage right and moves diagonally towards upstage left. He begins with a *chassé* (to the right foot), *tour jeté*, then a *chassé, demi-fouetté*. He is now facing downstage right with his left leg in *arabesque*. He runs two steps forward (left-right), then executes a *saut de basque*, followed by a *chassé* and double *saut de basque*. Another *chassé* leads to an *assemblé* with a double turn, landing in fifth position, from which he finishes the sequence with a double *tour en l'air*.

The *tour jeté* can be a sharp and impressive movement in classical ballet, and has counterparts in other forms of dance in which turns are combined with leaps. The *tour jeté* is particularly effective if the body appears to rise up from the floor, *then* flip over 180°, and finally return to earth. How is that illusion accomplished? And why is it an illusion? Why is it easier to accomplish the rotation for a *demi-fouetté*, for which the landing is on the same foot as the takeoff? How does one create the opposite illusion in the *saut de basque*, in which the body appears to *pause* in its rotation at the peak of the leap? What characteristics of the movement are important in achieving the angular velocity necessary for these turning leaps, especially in those cases in which a double turn is called for? How is the body coordinated so as to achieve the turn in the double *tour en l'air* so common in male variations in classical ballet? Also important is the question of how the rotation in each of these movements

Figure 5-1. Sean Lavery airborne in a scene from "Stars and Stripes." (Photo © 1983 Martha Swope)

is *ended* without coasting past the desired final position and orientation.

Each of these movements, like the *pirouettes* discussed in the last chapter, involves a rotation of all or part of the body around an axis. There are similarities and differences in the analyses that provide insights into the physical principles involved in these turning movements. Angular momentum is again the important quantity, since it must be constant during the time the body is in the air.

THE *TOUR JETE*

The *tour jeté* is a jump with a 180° turn, the dancer landing on the foot opposite to the takeoff foot. In this case Sean is facing the direction of motion when he takes off from

Figure 5-2.
Sean performing a *tour jeté*. Note that the rotation has begun while the legs are approaching each other, and stops when the moment of inertia is large in the final *arabesque* position aloft.

his right foot, and kicks a straight left leg into the air in front of him. After takeoff, his right leg moves up to meet the left, and he does a half turn to the right, landing on the left leg, right leg to the rear, and facing in the direction from which he came. The sequence of photographs in figure 5-2 shows Sean in consecutive stages of the *tour jeté* described.

Ballet dancers being taught this movement often hear an instruction something like, "Square your shoulders and hips! The turn is most brilliant when you rise straight up and then start to turn right at the peak of the jump!" When laws of physics are applied to such a model of the movement, one can quickly conclude that it must involve a violation of conservation of angular momentum. (See appendix B.) But if this movement is observed performed

by an accomplished dancer, one does indeed see the body apparently flipping in the air *after* contact with the ground has ended. How is this illusion created, and how can a dancer maximize the effectiveness of the illusion? Rhonda Ryman has provided some insights into this movement.[1]

There is clearly some angular momentum associated with this turn in the air. But there can be no angular momentum unless there has been some torque acting on the body. Once the body has lost contact with the floor there is no longer a source of torque, so whatever angular momentum existed at the moment of takeoff is maintained throughout the flight phase of the movement. The torque must be exerted against the floor before takeoff, so that the turning motion is established. But when the foot leaves the floor the body has a large moment of inertia (see appendix B), meaning that the body's mass is distributed far from the axis of rotation. The left foot is extended to the front, the right foot has just left the floor to the rear, and the arms are in front of the body moving up. Since the angular momentum is equal to the product of the moment of inertia and the angular velocity, the large moment of inertia produces a small rotation rate. That is, when the body mass is spread far from the axis of rotation, the rate of rotation is small. But there *is* some rotation, as seen in the second view of Sean's *tour jeté* in figure 5-2, in which his body has turned somewhat as he approaches the peak of the jump.

At the peak of the jump, the legs cross close to each other along the axis of rotation, and the arms simultaneously come together overhead, also close to the axis of rotation. Thus the moment of inertia is decreased substantially at that time, and the rate of rotation increases accordingly. The appearance to an observer is that the body has suddenly acquired the turning motion at the peak of the jump! Upon landing, the arms open to the side and the right leg extends to the rear in

[1]Rhonda Ryman, "Classical Ballet Technique: Separating Fact from Fiction," *York Dance Review 5*, (1976):16. See also, by the same author, "A Kinematic and Descriptive Analysis of Selected Classical Ballet Skills," Master of the Arts thesis, Graduate Programme in Interdisciplinary Studies, York University, Toronto, January, 1976.

arabesque, thus increasing the moment of inertia again, and slowing the turn rate.

This analysis provides some clues to the dancer as to how to maximize the illusion of turning sharply at the peak of the jump. The legs must cross close to each other and the arms must come overhead *at the time the jump has reached its peak* in order to accomplish the decrease in moment of inertia at that moment, with the associated increase in turn rate. The body must approach as closely as possible a straight line configuration so that the mass is close to the longitudinal rotation axis. Note from the photograph of the *tour jeté* (figure 5-2) that the axis is inclined somewhat from the vertical at the peak of the jump when the rotation is occurring.

It is important to note that these physical characteristics of the *tour jeté* that are necessary for the illusion of flipping over at the peak of the jump are also consistent with the aesthetic requirements of the movement when that illusion is desired. But the reasons for those characteristics are now seen to be based not only on aesthetics but also on compatibility with physical principles that must apply to the movement.

A form of *tour jeté* that emphasizes a different aspect of the movement will be described after the discussion of the *demi-fouetté* in the next section.

THE *DEMI-FOUETTÉ*

The *demi-fouetté* is also a jump with a half turn, but in this case the left leg, which kicks to the front as the right foot leaves the floor, remains oriented towards the direction of motion while the body flips through its 180° rotation. The landing is on the right leg. In this case very little torque needs to be exerted against the floor, because the gesture leg, in which most of the moment of inertia resides, maintains its direction in space. Only the torso, head, and arms must revolve around the axis of rotation during the turn in the air.

In fact, suppose this movement is carried out with *no* torque against the floor. In this case the total angular momentum of the body remains zero, still allowing part of the body to rotate one direction while another part rotates the opposite direction. The torso, head, and arms can rotate a full half turn to the right, while the gesture leg revolves to the left. The movement of the extended gesture leg will be small, since its moment of inertia is large. An approximation to a good *demi-fouetté* can be carried out in this way. (This technique is a part of the complicated movements a cat executes when righting itself in the air after being dropped upside down.)

We can now return to another form of the *tour jeté* that emphasizes an aspect of the movement different from the illusion of flipping in the air described earlier. It also applies a different physical principle. In this case the gesture leg kicks to the front, and the torso, head, and arms turn *while* the moment of inertia of the legs is large, as in a *demi-fouetté*. After the torso has turned through 180°, the legs are reversed through a scissors motion so that the landing is again to the foot opposite to the takeoff foot. In this form of the movement the body flips to an *arabesque* position in the air very early, and then the legs reverse position. The impression is that the upper body floats down gracefully after the quick turning motion is completed.

THE *SAUT DE BASQUE*

The two running steps now lead to the *saut de basque*, another jumping turn. (Hannah Wiley has carried out a comprehensive study of the *saut de basque*.[2]) The right foot is again the push-off foot, and the left leg kicks forward in the direction of motion. In this movement, however, the body initially turns one-quarter turn to the right so that the left leg, still extended in the direction of motion, is now extended to the side of the body in second position, and the dancer now has his back to the audience. (The arms are also extended to the sides at that time.) As the dancer approaches a landing on the left foot, his body

[2]Hannah Wiley, "Laws of Motion Controlling Dance Movement: A Qualitative and Kinematic Analysis of *Saut de Basque*," Master's thesis, New York University School of Education, Health, Nursing, and Arts Professions, August, 1981.

rotates to the right to a position facing the audience, with the right leg in a *coupé* position in front of the ankle of the left leg. This movement is illustrated in the sequence of photographs of Sean in figure 5-3.

The jump in this movement involves the same principles discussed in chapter 3. The height of the jump is enhanced by the transfer of horizontal linear momentum to the vertical direction. That transfer must be controlled so that the linear motion is stopped at the end of the movement, or some motion is retained if the following movement continues traveling. The height of the jump must, of course, be sufficient to accomplish the turning motion while in the air, although the landing must be made slightly *before* the body faces the audience so that the supporting foot can exert the torque against the floor required to decrease the angular momentum back to zero.

As we have seen before, once the body leaves the floor there is no more torque, and the angular momentum must be a constant until landing. The torque must be exerted by the takeoff foot before it leaves the floor. (There is no possibility of a torque from *both* feet, since the two feet are not in contact with the floor at the same time in the running steps preceding the jump.) Note the importance of full foot contact with the floor during the jump so that the moment arm for the force couple is as large as possible. When the heel leaves the floor, very little torque can be exerted by the small area of the foot remaining in contact.

When the legs and arms are extended the moment of inertia is large, and the body seems to pause in its rotation—an important aspect in a well-executed *saut de basque*. As the left leg is brought down in preparation for the landing, and the arms and right leg are brought in closer to the body, the moment of inertia decreases significantly, and the body turns rapidly. The landing, with the retarding torque exerted by the supporting foot, completes the *saut de basque* turn. Again it is important to lower the left heel to the floor so that the full length of the foot is involved in the retarding torque.

Note that *too much* momentum will make it difficult to stop the turn at the end, since there is only one foot on the floor at that time that can exert the retarding torque

Figure 5-3.
Sean performing a *saut de basque* jumping turn. Note that the body turns little until the right leg comes in to the *retiré* position, which decreases the total moment of inertia.

against the floor. The timing of the pause with arms and leg extended is crucially important. If they remain extended for too long a time, the faster rotation that occurs after they are retracted will not occur before the landing. If the arms and leg are brought in too soon, there will be too much rotation with the smaller moment of inertia, and the movement will not end facing the audience.

The double *saut de basque* is usually performed without the pause with extended arms and left leg. The reason is clear. In order to accomplish two full turns (actually one and three quarters), the moment of inertia must be kept as small as possible so that the rotation rate is sufficiently large to accomplish the angular movement during the time in the air. The right leg may be in a *retiré* or *coupé* position during the turn, so that when the left leg is in *plié* after landing, the right leg does not drop to the floor. Figure 5-4 shows Sean near the peak of a

Figure 5-4. In a double *saut de basque* turn, the moment of inertia must be kept small throughout the movement in order for the necessary rate of turn to be maintained. The position shown here, rather than the extended position seen in figure 5-3, is maintained through most of the double turn.

double *saut de basque*, in which his body is much closer to the axis of rotation as he rotates than is the case with the "spread" position near the peak of the single turn.

THE TURNING *ASSEMBLÉ*

The next *chassé* is followed by a turning *assemblé*. This turn is similar to the *saut de basque* except that now the legs are straight and close to vertical, and the landing is made to both feet. The arms are usually overhead during the turn. In this case the moment of inertia is quite small, since the body mass is as close to the axis of rotation as is possible. The turn can be quite rapid, and double turns are easier than the double *saut de basque*.

One aspect of the turning *assemblé* is worth noting. If the moment of inertia is small at the *beginning* of the movement, while the takeoff foot is exerting the torque against the floor, it will be difficult to acquire sufficient angular momentum. The body will rotate away from its initial direction too rapidly to allow the torque to have its effect in producing the angular momentum. It will be difficult to accomplish the double turn during the time in the air, because the turn rate cannot be significantly increased after takeoff. If the moment of inertia is larger at the beginning, then it can be decreased after takeoff, thereby speeding the turn.

Although the left leg may extend somewhat during the initial phase, the arms are most important. The arms should extend and begin rotating in the direction of the turn before contact with the floor is lost, thereby absorbing much of the angular momentum generated by the torque at the foot *before* the body rotates very far. The arms then move to the overhead position, and the angular momentum resides in the whole body as it turns.

If the landing is in fifth position, the feet are close together, and exerting torque to *stop* the turn is difficult. It is again necessary to land before the turn is completed, allowing the body to slow to a stop in the desired direction.

THE *TOUR EN L'AIR*

In the sequence described at the beginning of this chapter, the turning *assemblé* is followed immediately by a double *tour en l'air*. Thus the angular momentum from the preceding motion can be retained, making the *tour* smoother. Retaining some of the angular momentum in this brief moment between jumps can be accomplished by allowing the arms to extend and continue their rotation. The angular momentum then resides in the arms while the legs, torso, and head remain facing the audience.

The double *tour en l'air* is most commonly performed with the body compacted as close to the vertical axis of rotation as possible, in order to maximize the angular velocity while the body is in the air. The legs are straight and vertical, and the arms are close in front of the body. The head spots twice during the double turn. Although the preparation for a *tour en l'air* normally has the feet in fifth position, many dancers find that the moment arm for the torque against the floor is too small, and that "cheating" by separating the feet somewhat in fourth or second position (separated front/back or side to side, respectively) makes the turn easier. Of course this movement is best learned by trying to accomplish the turn from a good fifth position, since the ideal can be approached if not achieved.

Either of two aspects of the *tour en l'air* may be emphasized when performing this movement. The horizontal forces exerted by the feet against the floor produce the torque that results in the angular momentum for the turn. The vertical force exerted by the feet produces the height of the jump that allows the body time to rotate. Emphasizing the horizontal forces will produce a rapid turn, while jumping higher and sacrificing horizontal force will produce a slower turn with more time in which to complete two full revolutions.

Of course the horizontal forces exerted by the feet against the floor must be a force *couple*, involving two equal and opposite forces, in order to produce a rotation with no horizontal acceleration away from the initial position. A common error is to distort the body somewhat (buttocks displaced towards the back, for instance) in the *plié* immediately preceding the jump. The effect is to throw the body off balance with the net horizontal force that results from such a distortion at the time of push-off.

Any movement that ends in a static position must involve some forces or torques that remove the momentum associated with the movement. When the *tour en l'air* is completed to a static position, the feet must have sufficient friction with the floor to exert the retarding torque necessary. Thus again the body should return to the floor before completion of the turn so that it may coast to a stop facing the audience. If the moment of inertia is increased (by extending the arms, for instance) as the body coasts to a stop, the rotation rate decreases so that there is little turning after landing. The decreased turn rate at the end makes the direction the body is facing when landing less critical than if the body were continuing its rapid rotation.

SUMMARY

All of the turns described in this chapter have involved the torques, angular velocities, and angular momenta also used in dealing with *pirouettes*. The jump has added some complications because of the combination of two kinds of motion. But the power of the physical analyses is particularly evident as these more complicated and spectacular movements succumb to careful treatment.

An effective *tour jeté* involves an illusion that requires controlling the rotation rate while in the air. The legs and arms must be brought as close as possible to the straight line around which the body is rotating at the time the peak of the jump is reached. This allows the rotation rate to increase drastically at that time, creating the illusion of flipping over at the peak of the movement. The *demi-fouetté*, while similar to the *tour jeté*, requires less angular momentum, and hence less torque, since the gesture leg maintains its orientation in space rather than revolving.

The *saut de basque* involves a similar control of the turn rate in the air, but this time the body is *extended* at the peak of the jump so as to create the illusion of *pausing* briefly in the turn. Since the takeoff and landing both involve just one foot, the accelerating and slowing torques require the full foot to be on the floor, maximizing the effectiveness of the feet in exerting the required torques. The double *saut de basque* turn eliminates the "pause," because the body must remain compact in order to maintain the turn rate required for two full turns before landing.

The turning *assemblé* and the *tour en l'air* both require a careful control of the moment of inertia of the body. It must be as large as feasible before takeoff so that the turn is relatively slow while torque is being exerted against the floor. After takeoff, the moment of inertia is decreased to provide a rapid turn rate. The arms, in addition to contributing to a large moment of inertia when they are extended at the beginning of the movement, also absorb much of the initial angular momentum by rotating relative to the body at the beginning of the turn. When in the air, the whole body shares the total angular momentum. In both of these turns, the landing must be made before the turn is completed, so that the body can coast to its final orientation while slowing to a stop. The slowing can only result from the retarding torque exerted by the feet against the floor.

A low, rapid turn is created by emphasizing the horizontal force couple exerted by the feet against the floor, while a high jump without so fast a turn results from emphasizing the vertical force. The proper emphasis will, of course, depend on the rhythm and the character of the choreography.

Turns in styles of dance other than classical ballet will also involve the control of the important mechanical parameters of the movement—angular velocity, body position and configuration, and the appropriate accelerating and decelerating torques against the floor. The physical analyses of this chapter can be applied to any turns for which the characteristics are sufficiently identified and understood.

CHAPTER 6

Effects of Body Size

Although height is a distinct asset when partnering tall women, tall dancers are well aware of the disadvantages of their height and long legs. *Adagio* movements may appear smoother when performed by a tall person, but *allegro* movements require considerably more strength than the same movements, to the same music, performed by shorter dancers.

Suppose the choreography now calls for Sean to perform a series of vertical jumps with beats of the legs (*entrechat quatre* and *entrechat six*) to a rather rapid tempo of the music. He must then accelerate quickly to the side into a *glissade assemblé* ending with a multiple *pirouette en dehors*.

Let's suppose that Sean, who is over six feet tall, has an understudy who is five feet, three inches, and is attempting the same choreography. How much more difficult are jumps and *entrechats* for tall people than short people, and why? Why is it that tall dancers have more difficulty getting the feet pointed or clearing the ground sufficiently to perform the required movements? How much more strength does the tall dancer require to perform the same movements as the shorter dancer in the same tempo? What special problems do horizontal accelerations and *pirouettes* present for the large dancer?

Dance teachers are particularly aware of differences between children and adults in the performance of dance movement. Although adults often have better developed muscles, coordination, and understanding, one often notices children performing certain types of movements

Figure 6-1. Children dance in a scene from the New York City Ballet's "Nutcracker." (Photo © 1983 Martha Swope)

more easily. Dance students undergoing a growth spurt in their early teen years usually experience a temporary loss of grace and body coordination. And choreographers are often aware that they must have different expectations of large and small dancers in terms of line, tempo of music, and general style of movement.

What are the physical bases of these effects of body size on the execution of dance movements? It is well known that accelerating a large mass requires a larger force than changing the velocity of a small mass at the same rate. But some of the more subtle "scaling" problems are not so obvious.

HEIGHT OF A VERTICAL JUMP

First let us consider vertical jumps. Much of this analysis applies to any jumps, whether in ballet, modern dance, or even non-dancing activities. In the particular choreography described above there is vertical motion *plus* beats with the legs while in the air. We will deal with the vertical motion first and then the beats. In chapter 3 the relationship between time in the air and the height of a jump was discussed. (A more detailed analysis is provided in appendix A.) We have seen that if the time allowed for the jump is short, a dancer with long feet may be unable to point his feet during the jump. This failure to accomplish what a smaller person could do with ease has nothing to do with skill or effort, but is a limitation imposed by laws of nature over which the dancer has absolutely no control!

Another implication of the relationship between time and height for a jump is that dancers of different sizes must jump the same absolute height off the floor in order to perform to the same tempo. If the tempo is slow, the shorter dancer may not be able to jump sufficiently high to "fill" the music, which leads to an apparent jerkiness. But there is another aspect of the jump that creates a *disadvantage* for the tall dancer. Part of an observer's impression of the height of a jump depends on its height *relative to the dancer's height*. That is, for a jump taking one-half second in the air, the jump height of about one foot may be one-quarter the body height of a short dancer, but only one-sixth that of a tall dancer. Such a jump is just not as impressive looking for the tall dancer. Again, there is nothing the tall dancer can do to extend his jump height without taking a longer time and lagging behind the music.

Figure 6-2 shows Sean with an extemporaneous "understudy" (the author's daughter), who is close to the five feet, three inches referred to earlier. In this case the taller Sean jumps to about the same proportion of his height as the shorter Virginia (in the second photo), but clearly, as shown in the last view, arrives back at the floor later than the shorter dancer.

Now let's consider the strength required to support or move a larger body. We've all noticed how a skinny-legged spider easily carries more than its own weight, or a flea is able to jump many times its own height, while the fat legs of an elephant hardly do more than support the animal itself. The reason can be understood by imagining two geometrically similar animals, one of which has exactly the same shape (the same body proportions) as the other but is twice as large in each linear dimension. The volume, and hence the mass, of the body is proportional to the third power of the linear dimension; the larger body thus has a weight eight times that of the smaller one. But the cross sectional area of the legs supporting the body depends on only the *second* power of the linear dimension, so that the larger animal has only four times the leg area. Thus the larger animal is supporting eight times the weight on four times the area, resulting in double the stress or pressure on the leg structure.

Excess stress or pressure on the body is responsible for injuries, which is one reason small people suffer fewer injuries. Of course young people have more flexibility in bones and tissues, also contributing to their resilience.

An important effect of size is the force a muscle can exert, which is roughly proportional to the cross sectional area of the total packet of fibers in a particular muscle. If this larger animal has muscles twice the linear size of the smaller one, the muscles would have four times

Figure 6-2. A short and a tall dancer, jumping to a height about the same proportion of their own height, will be in the air different lengths of time. Here the author's daughter Virginia acts as Sean Lavery's "understudy," and arrives at the floor before Sean, who jumped higher.

the cross sectional area and could exert four times the force. But if the mass to be accelerated is eight times as great, the larger animal is going to have more difficulty in its movements, and must exert more muscular effort to move at the same rate as the smaller one.

How do these scaling principles apply to dancers? Suppose a young male dancer is five feet, three inches tall, while Sean is just over six feet (15% taller). Further, suppose their bodies are identically shaped (same proportions). Sean will weigh about 52% more than Shorty, and will have muscles 32% stronger. Thus in order to jump to a height of one foot, taking one-half second, Sean must exert 15% more muscular effort. In order to jump to a height about one-fifth of his own height (a one-foot jump

for Shorty), Sean must jump about 1.2 feet and exert 32% more muscular effort than the shorter dancer.

Consider the energy required for this movement, which is directly related to the number of calories burned in the process of moving the body. The physical work done in a vertical jump is the product of the weight and the height, and thus is 52% more for Sean than for Shorty. If each jumps to the same *proportion of his own height*, Sean expends about 75% more energy!

ENTRECHATS

Now let us consider the beats with the legs that Sean must perform while in the air during his jump. These beats are oscillating rotations of the leg around a horizontal axis through the hip joint. A torque is required at the hip in order to produce the angular acceleration (see appendix B). In order for *entrechats* to be accomplished in the same tempo and with the same angular amplitude by both Sean and Shorty, the angular accelerations of the legs will be the same for both of them. As shown in appendix B, the torque required is proportional to the moment of inertia, which depends not only on the mass, but on the square of the distance of the mass from the rotation axis. (The contributions from the individual parts of the leg at their distances from the hip must be added.) Thus the moment of inertia of a leg is proportional to the fifth power of its linear size. Sean's leg has 101% more moment of inertia than Shorty's (about double), and Sean must exert *double* the torque to produce the same angular acceleration, and hence the same leg motion in the same tempo.

Other factors make the problem less severe. Sean's muscles, being 32% fatter in cross-sectional area, can exert 32% more force for the same "effort." And the structure of the joint, including the distance from the center of the joint to the point of muscle attachment to the bone, is also bigger in Sean. This allows a particular muscle force to produce more torque. The final result is that Sean must still exert 32% more muscular "effort" to perform beats at the same rate as his smaller counterpart.

How about the energy expended doing *entrechats?* Since the angular motion is assumed to be the same for the different bodies, the energy required is proportional to the torque. Thus Sean is expending energy at about *double* the rate as Shorty.

HORIZONTAL ACCELERATIONS AND BODY SIZE

Sean's next movement involves a quick horizontal acceleration away from his initial position. As we have seen in chapter 3, this acceleration is proportional to the horizontal friction force between the foot and the floor, and inversely proportional to the body's mass. Since the friction force is proportional to the weight, there is no advantage or disadvantage associated with size in realizing sufficient non-slipping friction force to accomplish a particular linear acceleration.

But how does the dancer achieve the off-balance condition necessary for a horizontal force and acceleration? These techniques, discussed in chapter 3, do involve slower processes for larger dancers. For instance, the toppling of the body from a vertical configuration to one of increasing angle with the vertical makes it possible to exert an increasing horizontal accelerating force against the floor. But the rate of topple is slower in direct proportion to the linear size. So it will take longer for a tall dancer to topple to an angle sufficient to exert the required horizontal accelerating force against the floor.

BODY SIZE AND *PIROUETTES*

Sean's final movement in this sequence is a multiple *pirouette en dehors*. Does he experience a disadvantage or advantage compared to a shorter person in performing this movement?

The moment of inertia of a body around any axis of rotation depends on the fifth power of the linear size of the body (assuming the same shape for bodies of different sizes). So Sean's moment of inertia around a vertical axis is double that of Shorty. Sean can exert 32% more force with his muscles (which are that much fatter than Shorty's). The horizontal forces of the feet against the floor, which produce the force couple that initiates the *pirouette*, are thus 32% greater for Sean. However, the same body position will produce a 15% larger distance between front and back feet in the preparatory position, so the accelerating torque will be 52% greater for Sean than Shorty. But we're then left with an angular acceleration 32% less for Sean than for Shorty, or else Sean must exert 32% more muscular effort than Shorty in order to perform the *pirouettes* at the same rate.

Now the frictional force at the floor is a problem.

When the shoe is not moving against the floor, the horizontal force between the two surfaces can be as great as $F = CW$, where C is the coefficient of static friction, and W is the body weight. Thus for a given coefficient of friction the friction force can be as great as 52% greater for Sean than for Shorty. The greater spread of feet in the preparatory position means that the torque can be as much as 75% greater for Sean. But in order to produce the same angular acceleration as Shorty, Sean must exert 101% greater torque. Thus the larger dancer may require a larger coefficient of friction—and consequently more rosin, for instance—to perform *pirouettes* at the same rate as a smaller dancer. Slipping of the feet at the beginning of a *pirouette* can be more of a problem for Sean than for Shorty.

ADAGIO MOVEMENTS

Most of the effects of size discussed here result in disadvantages for the large dancer. It is true, however, that slow movements sometimes look more graceful and smooth when performed by taller people. (One person is reported to have said, after watching *Swan Lake* performed by a company of small dancers, "After all, it's not supposed to be *Duck Lake!*")

One reason for the smoothness of movement possible for taller dancers involves the slower accelerations that result from the muscular effort of a large person. When Sean exerts 90% of his strength in a particular movement, his body responds with a corresponding acceleration. Shorty, to produce movement at the same rate, will exert perhaps 50% of his strength. It is probably easier to control the body smoothly when the exertion required is close to zero or close to maximum, and hardest halfway between where sizable variations in exerted strength are possible either direction from the magnitude required for the movement. Thus Shorty will have more difficulty moving smoothly at the slow tempo that requires less of his strength.

CHAPTER 7

Partnering

Some of the most beautiful moments in dance occur when a man and woman are dancing in sensitive partnership. A soloist depends only on individual self-controlled body movement; a partnership involves the extra dimension of communication with another person. A very different form of concentration is necessary in creating that communication effectively. The dancer must not only be sensitive to his or her own timing, balance, strength, body shape, and individual quirks of technique, but must also sense and adjust to those characteristics of the partner. When a partnership develops a mutual trust, sensitivity, and cooperation, the results can be breathtakingly beautiful. Karsavina and Nijinsky, Fonteyn and Nureyev, McBride and Villella, Farrell and Martins, Kirkland and Baryshnikov, and many more—all have created memorable moments on the stage of classical ballet.

Suppose Lisa and Sean embark on a *pas de deux*. The choreography calls for a series of short vertical lifts early in the sequence. An overhead lift and carry is followed by a descent into a balanced *arabesque* on *pointe* on her right leg. Sean moves to a position in front of Lisa as she faces stage right, and takes her right hand in his as he supports her pose, now an *attitude derrière*. This pose is to be maintained during a full turn clockwise promenade, reminiscent of the famous "Rose Adagio" section in Act II of *The Sleeping Beauty* ballet.

Finally there are the supported *pirouettes* that often occur near the end of a classical *pas de deux*. A series

Figure 7-1. Suzanne Farrell and Peter Martins in a scene from "Allegro Brillante." (Photo © 1983 Martha Swope)

Figure 7-2. Three couples in various stages of lifts, from "Histoire du Soldat." In the foreground are Kyra Nichols, Heather Watts, and Darci Kistler. Heather Watts's partner is Bart Cook. (Photo © 1983 Martha Swope)

of finger turns ends with a multiple-turn *pirouette* supported by Sean's hands at Lisa's waist. The final pose, with Lisa in *retiré* position, ends the sequence.

A number of questions arise in this brief *pas de deux*. What are the responsibilities of each of the partners in accomplishing the lifts? How can they develop the coordination that will allow both of them to use their strength most smoothly and effectively? How is the descent from a lift made sufficiently gentle to avoid injury? What is the appropriate role of each partner in maintaining balance in the supported pose and promenade? How do the partners cooperate in maintaining balance in the supported *pirouettes?* Who is responsible for the torque producing the turn for the *pirouette?* How does Sean provide the torque to stop the *pirouette*, or to maintain the turn in a finger turn?

Let us analyze the movements physically in order to find answers to these questions.

VERTICAL LIFTS

First let us consider the lifts. Contrary to appearance, a lift is not dependent entirely on the arm strength of the male dancer. His leg strength is at least as important, and the timing and coordination of the separate movements of male and female are crucially important. The short vertical lifts must be accomplished in the time allowed by the music, which can create some problems if significant height is desired. Many of the same principles applying to the vertical jumps discussed in chapter 3 also apply to vertical lifts. But here the descent must slow to a soft landing in order to avoid injury and an aesthetically unpleasing appearance.

The technique for a lift to a stable equilibrium position is different from that for a temporary lift in which the partner is only prolonging the duration of the time in the air. For a lift to a stable position, the center of gravity of the combination of the masses of the two people must be directly over the area of support. If the centers of gravity of both partners individually meet that condition, then not only is the force he exerts entirely vertical, but no torques are required. If her position is displaced from that vertical line, then there must be some torque (generally at his shoulders) to support her. (Imagine holding a weight directly overhead, or, with more difficulty, holding it directly in front of you.)

It is most difficult for a male dancer, even a strong one, to support his partner in equilibrium if she is displaced in position very far from the location over his area of support. Therefore the position for such stable

Figure 7-3. (*below*). Lisa de Ribère and Sean Lavery performing a stable lift, in which her center of gravity is almost directly above his center of supporting force from the floor.

Figure 7-4 (*at right*). Lisa and Sean performing a "temporary" lift, in which a sizable torque at his shoulders is necessary to support Lisa, whose center of gravity is displaced from the stable position over Sean's support at the floor.

lifts is generally directly overhead, in an inverted arched position or any other of a variety of positions. One such stable lift is shown in the photograph of Lisa and Sean in figure 7-3. A common lift *not* culminating in a stable position involves a straight vertical lift with the woman situated directly in front of her partner, both facing front, as illustrated in figure 7-4. She may perform *entrechats* while in the air, remaining upright. In order for her to accomplish the proper movements and position she must remain in front of her partner. If he tries to get her to a stable position overhead during this temporary lift she will either fold a bit in the middle or tangle her feet in his front side! His proper technique must be to thrust her a bit front near the top of the motion in order to maintain that clearance. This thrust also helps him straighten his arms at the top of the motion so that it is easier to hold her up and extend the time in the air.

Of course for proper technique in this lift, as in others, the lifter should delay straightening his legs until the arms are well on their way to being straight. The leg muscles are substantially stronger than the arm muscles, and can be used for much of the lifting. As the arms or the legs approach full straight extension, the force they can exert becomes larger. In the diagram shown in figure 7-5 below, the bent arm in the first case can only exert a quarter as much lifting force as in the second case, for the same torque at the elbow and shoulder. Therefore the arms should be brought to as straight a configuration as possible

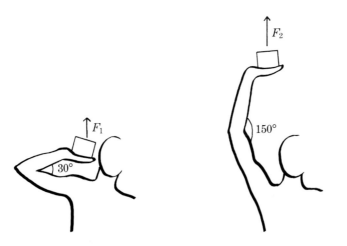

Figure 7-5.
When the arms are almost straight, a greater vertical force may be exerted. In the case shown here, the magnitude of the force F_2 is about four times the magnitude of F_1 for the same muscle force and torque at the elbow and shoulder.

while most of the upward impetus is coming from the woman's jump. As the momentum from her jump is expended, his arms and legs take over for the latter part of the lift. The lift then appears most smooth and flowing.

On the *descent* from any lift the woman can exert no upward force to help slow her motion as she approaches the floor until her feet touch and she starts retarding her downward motion while descending into a *plié*. If the descent is not into a *plié* it becomes even more important for her partner to be able to exert more upward force to slow the downward motion than was exerted on the way up. This is difficult because his arms are increasingly bent during the descent. So the legs must again be used, aided by friction against the body. A common technique for slowing the descent is for the male to allow his partner to slide down the front of his body to some extent, preventing that sudden arrival at the floor that can play havoc with her feet! We have all seen the descending ballerina's foot searching for the floor to prevent an awkward, unexpected, and potentially hazardous landing.

In general, lifts should maximize the effective use of the strength of both partners in order to accomplish that constant goal of apparent effortlessness. The woman must jump with strength, not depending on her partner to exert all the effort. Her partner must maximize the use of the legs, depend on his arms mostly when they are almost straight, and be conscious of the position of her center of gravity so as not to have to exert unnecessary effort.

Some interesting studies on lifting techniques have been carried out and reported by Tony Lycholat in a series of articles.[1] He concentrates on such characteristics as the distance between partners when the lift commences and the timing of the vertical forces.

BALANCE IN A POSE

Now consider the balance in *attitude*, with a promenade. Whereas a *soloist* in balance must depend only on the floor

[1]Tony Lycholat. "Lifting Technique in Dance—A Scientific Investigation," *Dancing Times*, November, 1982, p. 123; part II, December, 1982, pp. 203-4.

for the forces required to maintain balance, now the *partner* can act as a source of forces in addition to gravity and the floor. Of course there are many types of partner contact that affect the motion of the body. One is straightforward, involving just one additional contact between the dancer and her partner—a contact at one hand. Another, supported *pirouettes*, is more complicated, involving two hands, friction, and rotational motion. What is the appropriate role of each partner in maintaining the woman's balance in these partnership movements?

In considering this choreography, one is reminded of the well known "Rose Adagio" section of the "Sleeping Beauty," which involves the lead ballerina, Aurora, and four suitor princes. Part of the traditional choreography has Aurora, in *attitude derrière* on *pointe*, being supported by one hand by each of the princes in turn, once briefly between balanced poses, and once with a full promenade, as illustrated by Sean and Lisa in figure 7-6.

Partners often struggle with the appropriate technique for maintaining the balance. Since contact between the partners exists only at the one hand, it is not easy for Aurora to control her balance by controlling the forces exerted by that one hand. A common problem occurs when she twists away from her partner, no longer facing him, and distorts the graceful partner relationship intended by the choreographer. The job of maintaining balance is hers; her partner must act as a rigid support that she can push or twist against to maintain control over her position. How does she accomplish this control effectively? A physical analysis provides some valuable clues.

A ballerina in this balanced pose has two locations where forces can be applied—the hand and the supporting foot. Her center of gravity is approximately over her supporting foot. If her center of gravity is displaced to her side, the condition of balance is not met, and, unless corrective action is taken, she falls. Three actions are possible: First, the body can be moved in such a way that balance is restored with no dependence on the supporting hand; this situation was analyzed in chapter 3. Such a technique is often seen when a wavering ballerina stretches to prolong a slightly "off" final balance at the climax of the

adagio. The second technique is to apply a sideways force with the hand against the partner's hand. This force will clearly be translated into a net horizontal force on the center of gravity in a direction chosen to restore balance. The third possible action is to exert a twisting torque with the hand against the partner's hand. Note that the last two techniques avoid distortions of the body that would be necessary to regain balance without using the partner's hand.

Use of the hand to exert a sideways force not only applies a restoring force to the center of gravity to regain balance, but also has the unfortunate effect of producing a torque around the vertical axis through the supporting foot. This results in the dancer twisting away from her partner, leaving her hand no longer directly in front of her. Not only is the aesthetic form destroyed, but the hand is left in a position where it is more difficult to control the forces and torques. It is possible, though, to exert a *torque*, or *twist*, with the hand in such a way as to avoid a torque around the vertical axis through the supporting foot. This torque around the axis *passing through the hand* can be as effective as a lateral force in displacing the center of gravity back towards the balanced condition, but doesn't cause the undesirable and uncontrolled twist away from the partner. The details of this analysis are presented in appendix J.

One intriguing aspect of this analysis is that it makes sense out of instructions for the accepted technique. The dancer and her partner should both have the elbows raised and the hand horizontal (woman palm down and partner palm up), rather than in a position more like shaking hands. If the hand is vertical, it is possible to exert a substantial torque *inward* (palm toward the arm), but much more difficult in the other direction, in which the hand tends to pull away from that of the partner. Thus if the hands are not horizontal, the tendency is to exert

Figure 7-6. Supported *attitude derrière*, with promenade. Lisa must maintain balance with a twisting torque exerted at her partner's hand rather than with a lateral force.

a lateral force with the hand rather than a torque, resulting in the very common tendency to twist away from the partner.

So the balanced *attitude* can be made effective if Sean holds his hand strongly in the proper position, and Lisa makes sure she maintains balance by applying a torque against his hand rather than a sideways force. Only in that way can she remain facing him while holding her pose during the promenade.

A DIGRESSION—THE BARRE AS A PARTNER

Although this discussion may seem out of place in that barre exercises have nothing to do with partnering, the barre can be treated much as a "partner" for the purpose of an analysis of balance. The barre provides a source of force and torque in addition to the floor, which, in chapter 2, was the *only* source of force acting on the body. The analysis in the last section, which deals with balance in a pose with support from a partner, makes it clear that forces exerted against the partner's supporting hand must be carefully controlled in order to avoid causing unwanted movement.

A dancer should use the barre mostly to maintain balance by means of a light force with one hand, which allows for a concentration on positions, movements, and placement of the body during the barre exercises. When the dancer is in the "centre," the necessity to maintain balance without the aid of the barre is added to the other aspects of movement calling for concentrated mental and physical effort.

The barre *is* effective in making balance easier. But since the point of contact between the supporting hand and the barre is *not* over the supporting foot, and is therefore not on the vertical line through the center of gravity, a force exerted against the barre in an attempt to regain lost balance is likely to produce a twist of the body away from the desired direction in addition to a displacement of the center of gravity back towards the proper balance position. The effectiveness of a *torque* rather than a force exerted against the barre follows from the analysis of the comparable situation of the supported pose with a partner, described in the last section.

Some barre movements involving turns must be handled very carefully. If the barre is used as a source of torque producing the angular momentum for the turn, there is a strong tendency for the dancer to be thrown off balance by the force against the barre. Examples of barre exercises involving turns include *fouetté* turns and *flic-flac* turns, in both of which the turning motion is produced by pushing longitudinally along the barre. But that longitudinal force along the barre not only provides a torque around the vertical rotation axis, but also results in a net horizontal force tending to throw the body off balance.

Suppose a dancer is standing with the right hand on the barre, and is preparing to perform a *fouetté* turn to the left. The left leg is extended to the front, and then a backwards force is exerted with the right hand against the barre as the leg starts rotating towards the left, giving the body the required angular momentum to rotate to the left. But that backwards force against the barre also produces a net horizontal acceleration of the body towards the *front*, if the body is initially balanced.

What does a dancer do to compensate for this unwanted linear acceleration towards the front? The most common technique involves a combination of two mechanisms. First, the body is placed so as to be slightly off balance to the rear just before the turn, so that the backwards force against the barre succeeds only in *returning* the center of gravity back to the balance position when the turn commences. Secondly, some of the torque is exerted by the supporting foot against the floor, so that the barre is not the only source of torque contributing to the turn.

These mechanisms do seem to work, but dancers and dance teachers should be aware that turning movements performed at the barre are actually quite different than when performed in the centre because of the complicating effects of the forces against the barre.

SUPPORTED *PIROUETTES*—BALANCE

Supported *pirouettes* are among the most prevalent components of choreography for partners in classical ballet. Seldom does one see a *pas de deux* that does not include the ballerina performing *pirouettes*, her partner behind her with hands on her waist, helping maintain her balance and control the turn. What is each partner's job in this instance of shared responsibility? How do the appropriate forces for maintaining her balance differ depending on whether she is stationary or turning?

First suppose the ballerina is in a non-rotating *pirouette* position (supporting leg straight, on *pointe*, with the gesture leg raised to the side with its foot at the knee of the supporting leg). It is clear that if her center of gravity is displaced horizontally from that region directly above the small area of support at the floor, the partner merely has to exert a force at her waist in the appropriate direction to return her to a balanced position. If she meantime is trying to regain her own balance by the techniques described in chapter 2, she is making her partner's job most difficult. One of the hardest jobs for a woman learning to be partnered is to prevent herself from doing those balance-regaining body manipulations that are so important when she is dancing solo.

Suppose now that she is rotating. Again she must not try to maintain her own balance once the turn has begun. Her partner's job, however, is still made more difficult by the rotation. There is generally a friction force between her waist and the partner's hands. (If her waist were frictionless, the situation would be little different from the non-rotating case in terms of balance, but there would be problems controlling the turn!) The partner's hands will exert a force into her waist, plus a friction force parallel to the surface, opposite to the direction of sliding motion. If she is balanced while turning, the lateral forces exerted by the partner's two hands would be equal and opposite, producing no net force on her, as shown in figure 7-7a. If she is turning to the right, his right hand would be exerting some force to the left, plus a friction force acting opposite to the motion, or towards

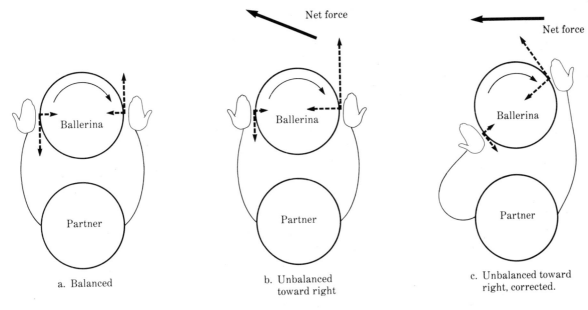

Figure 7-7. Hand positions for supported *pirouettes*, viewed from above.

the front. His left hand would be exerting some force to the right, plus a friction force towards the back.

Now suppose the ballerina is off balance towards stage right while she is turning to the right. If her partner exerts a greater force with the right hand towards stage left (the natural tendency), there would indeed be an appropriate correcting response of her body to the left. However, because his right hand is pushing harder against her waist than his left, there will be a greater friction force at the right hand than the left, as shown in figure 7-7b. Thus there will be an unwanted movement of her position towards the front in addition to the correcting response to the left. The partner's job, then, is to be sensitive to the magnitude of the friction force, and adjust his right-hand position somewhat to the front so that its force is directed more to the back, counteracting the effect of the friction force towards the front, as shown in figure 7-7c.

The difficulty in supporting a *pirouette* can be seen when one observes inexperienced students. If the woman is not reasonably close to balance in the *pirouette*, large correcting forces are required of the partner. Unless the adjustment in direction of force is made as described above, there is a strong tendency for the partner's correcting forces to be ineffective in maintaining her balance. In the above example, if the hand position is not shifted to that shown in figure 7-7c, she would tend to fall forward, and her partner, belatedly adjusting the hand position to the front, but having to increase the force, finds his arm wrapping around her, stopping the *pirouette* at an unexpected time and position. The results can be amusing, as the two try to extricate themselves from this entanglement with his arm surrounding her, perhaps trapping her arms in unlikely and not very graceful positions!

A turn to the right, unbalanced to the left, produces the opposite problem. What is the effect of the friction force that results when the left hand pushes harder to the right to correct the imbalance? Referring again to the diagrams, we see that there will be a net force to the *right* and *back*, causing her to be shifted to the right but also towards her partner. In fact, in the extreme case, she rolls right up his left arm, again bringing the *pirouette* to a grinding halt in strange, awkward, and unexpected configurations!

An experienced ballerina will usually perform the *pirouettes* close to a balanced position so that only subtle forces are necessary from the partner. An experienced partner will be sensitive to slight imbalances so that he can adjust the hand positions and force directions quickly enough to prevent disaster. In fact, if the ballerina is slightly off balance to the rear, the best appearance is attained, because her partner's hands can remain slightly in back of her, shifting positions as necessary without moving in front of her in clear view of the audience. He never has to have a hand in front to pull her back, a movement that can compromise the aesthetic appearance of the *pirouette*.

All dancers, even those most talented and accomplished, have experienced a supported *pirouette* fraught with potential disaster. Large corrections are extremely difficult for the male partner, requiring strength and

Figure 7-8. Lisa and Sean in valiant attempts to perform a
supported *pirouette* sufficiently off balance to make clear the
corrective hand positions required. The second case portrays one of
those dreaded disasters one hopes never to encounter on stage!

counter-intuitive responses. Professionals can be distin-
guished from inexperienced dancers not so much by their
avoidance of such problems, but by their avoidance of
any interruption in the sense of movement and aesthetic
projection while they attempt to solve the problems.
The resulting smoothness and flow allow the audience
to see *dance* as opposed to feats of physical prowess.
Lisa and Sean, being the artists they are, struggled to
perform the *pirouettes* sufficiently *off* balance to demonstrate the problems described here. The results, as shown
in figure 7-8, were sometimes amusing! For the most

part, however, they preserved beautiful fluidity of movement in spite of these constraints.

SUPPORTED *PIROUETTES*—CONTROL OF ROTATION

While Lisa is performing her supported *pirouettes*, Sean must be concentrating not only on her balance, but also on helping her control the rate of turn. What is the male partner's responsibility for initiating, maintaining, or stopping a supported *pirouette?* How can he exert the appropriate torques for these motions? The forces and torques required to control the turn must be carried out at the same time as those required for maintaining balance as discussed above.

The common supported *pirouette* was described above and analyzed in terms of the forces required by the partner to keep the ballerina balanced. The partner can also help control the turn by providing some additional torque with his hands to help initiate a stronger turn or keep a turn rotating in rhythm with the music, or provide a strong *retarding* torque to stop the turn at the right position and time.

One often sees at the climax of a *pas de deux* (as in the *Nutcracker pas de deux* near the end of the ballet) a series of supported *pirouettes*, each multiple turn ending in a pose *en face*. Because a dancer on *pointe* has little friction, and a rapid turn has substantial angular momentum, it can be difficult for her to control a rapid or repeated *pirouette* without help from her partner. Only with the partner's help, for instance, can she stop in a pose while still on *pointe*, since there is no other means for her to get rid of her angular momentum. How does a partner exert the appropriate torques to control the turn while also exerting those forces with his hands that keep his partner balanced?

A retarding torque to stop a *pirouette* is not difficult. Increasing the force of the hands into the waist will increase the friction force, thus slowing the turn as rapidly as desired. It may appear that the ballerina helps by opening the arms as the *pirouette* ends, thereby increasing the moment of inertia and decreasing the turn rate. But

Figure 7-13. Two phases of a finger turn in which Sean's hand is moving in a circle as shown in Figure 7-12.

This mechanism, pictured in the diagram in figure 7-12, is similar to the action used when swinging a weight on a string in a circle around the head.

Figure 7-13 shows Sean exerting the torque on Lisa that maintains her rotation in the finger turn. The two instants shown demonstrate the circular motion of his hand that produces the appropriate forces on her hand.

SUMMARY

The partners in this sequence of movements have been concerned with lifts, balance, and *pirouettes*. The lifts are of two types: those in which the woman's center of gravity is above her partner's area of support on the floor so that he does not have to exert a torque to keep her in position, and those lifts of shorter duration in which she is usually in front of him. Any lift must involve coordination of her jump with his lift, and is made smoother if he uses his legs for as much of the lifting movement as possible, rather than his arms. Doing so usually means straightening the arms *before* straightening the legs, which are stronger. The legs and arms both are strongest when they are close to straight, so the lift should be coordinated so that the maximum force is needed when the limbs are almost straight.

When a woman is balancing in a pose with support from a partner, it is *her* job to maintain balance, and his to keep the supporting hand in a solid position. If she exerts a lateral force on his hand in order to correct for imbalance, she will rotate away from him. It is important for her to correct by means of a twisting *torque*, instead. The hand position (palms horizontal) makes this torque easier.

Contrary to the case of the balanced pose, it is the woman's *partner* who bears the responsibility for maintaining her balance in a *pirouette*, once she is rotating. If she tries to help maintain her own balance, it makes his job harder. That job is hard enough, since the orientation of his hands, and the direction of the applied forces of his hands on her waist, must change depending on the direction of imbalance that must be corrected. The frictional characteristics of the hand/waist contact also are important in determining the appropriate location and force from his hands.

That contact friction also is important as he controls her rate of turn, which must involve torques exerted at her waist to change her angular momentum. Slowing the turn is not difficult, since increasing pressure will produce a retarding force couple at her waist. *Increasing* her angular momentum is more difficult, and must involve a careful placement of the hands.

A finger turn requires a steady supporting hand above the woman's head to act as a pivot. This turn can be maintained through many rotations by moving the supporting hand in a circular motion so as to exert a torque to keep the woman rotating. Clearly this lateral force at the overhead pivot would destroy her balance if she were initially balanced, so she actually must be slightly off balance in order to experience an accelerating torque.

When all of these aspects of partnering are worked out and the problems are understood and solved, Sean and Lisa are able to forget about the analysis and concentrate on dancing. The results can be exhilarating to both the dancers and the audience!

The Future

No one would dispute the claim that the scientific study of dance is in its infancy as a serious endeavor. Physics has been around for centuries, and dance for as long as human beings have tried to interpret their experience through movement. Since physics deals with the properties and causes of movement, why have the two areas not contributed to each other more fruitfully? For what reasons might we see a change in this situation on the horizon?

The application of biomechanics to sport is a lively and accepted field. Why has dance not progressed in a parallel way? One answer lies in the fact that quality of performance in sport is quantifiable, while in dance the judgment of quality depends on aesthetic interpretation. What we are finding recently, however, is that a lack of understanding of applicable physical principles imposes constraints and limitations on dancers in a similar, but not identical, way that athletes are limited. A dancer who can attain extra height from a jump, a sharper turn in a *tour jeté*, or a smoother landing from a *tour en l'air* has more tools to work with, and more flexibility with which to achieve aesthetic goals.

As the scientific study of dance expands in the future, it can take different directions. Increasing numbers of researchers are studying particular movements in detail, using modern technical tools such as high-speed cinematography and computer analysis. This is certainly a useful direction, and such studies will form a foundation

Figure 8-1. Judith Jamison and Mikhail Baryshnikov in "Pas de Duke." (Photo © 1983 Martha Swope)

on which teachers, dancers, and other researchers can build a better understanding of dance both for the sake of the pure understanding itself and for the improvement of dance technique. Those studies *must*, however, be complemented by overviews of the role of physical analysis in understanding dance. This role will include qualitative analyses of many different movements, with the emphasis on understanding what basic physical principles are applicable, how the body functions within the constraints of these physical laws, and what connections exist between different movements in dance and in other types of human body movement. We must not lose the "forest" of a broad physical context as we investigate the "trees" of individual movement analyses. This broader approach has been the emphasis in this book.

The time is ripe for expanding our involvement with dance analysis. Traditionally dancers (particularly ballet dancers) have begun their training at an age too young to grasp the abstraction of physical principles applied to human body movement. By the time the mind has matured in its analytical capacities, dancers have established dance in their minds as an activity learned and motivated more by instinct, feeling, and the copying of models than by questioning and analysis. But children are now growing up in a world that more readily accepts analytical approaches to a variety of human endeavor, from economics to politics, from literature to music. People are rapidly discovering the immense potential usefulness of computers and other technical tools for contributing to our knowledge in a wide variety of fields. Children are increasingly exposed to analytical ways of thinking. Some will reject these approaches as being a necessary evil for "others" to cope with, and some will accept and use the approaches comfortably. In this increasing dichotomy, should dancers be expected to be entirely of the former type, or will some see the natural benefit of an analytical approach to creative and aesthetic arts?

How can dancers and others deeply involved with dance use this new awareness in ways that contribute to the art form and not detract from it? First they must be open to the ideas—willing to see the possible usefulness.

Figure 8-2. New York City Ballet's "Serenade." (Photo © 1983 Martha Swope)

These analyses can provide, for instance, a much deeper understanding of the causal connections between different aspects of dance movement. If a dancer has some problem with the trajectory of flight in a jumping movement, knowing that the trajectory of a body in the air is totally determined by interactions with the floor *before* takeoff can allow attention to be focused on the takeoff rather than the flight phase of the movement.

Dance teachers will increasingly find that this type of understanding, rather than replacing existing techniques, can complement present teaching methods. *Some* students will respond well to this deeper approach, and some will not. But teachers will have additional tools at their disposal with which to help students learn dance.

The danger that dance will become too analytical, and the emphasis will shift towards athletic accomplishments rather than aesthetic quality, has been with us as long as there have been observers of dance who are not sensitive to its artistic dimensions. But the traditions of dance have always been strong enough to withstand this danger. There are also those who are uncomfortable with these new approaches and are threatened by them. Perhaps these people will be drawn into the ideas as they become convinced they can be useful and not damaging. It is a responsibility of all who *are* involved in this work that the ideas be brought constantly to earth, and that connections to the world of real flesh-and-blood dancers be constantly maintained.

Where can people go who are interested in learning more about physical analyses of dance movement? Much of the literature in this area now is oriented towards a pure understanding, rather than towards applications to improvement of technique. As more people become involved, particularly those who have experience in the teaching of dance, these analyses will be brought into the traditions of dance instruction. An increasing number of workshops, conferences, and publications will be dealing with these analyses. The *Kinesiology for Dance* Newsletter,[1] for example, is an informal publication with an expanding coverage and circulation.

Meanwhile, we can look forward with great anticipation to the progress in the art form of dance that can result from a marrying of the technical and the aesthetic, the rational and the emotional—the mind and the body!

CHAPTER 8:
THE FUTURE

[1]Contact the author for current information about this publication.

Linear Mechanics and Newton's Laws

Mechanics is a study of the properties of motion of massive objects in response to forces. The description of motion itself is called kinematics, involving relationships between position, velocity, acceleration, and time. Dynamics, on the other hand, involves the relationships between motion and the causes of changes of motion. Let us first define the terms associated with kinematics.

Position is a description of the location of a point representing a particle or some specific point in an extended object. Position can be described in one dimension (along a line such as the vertical line important in describing the characteristics of vertical jumps), two dimensions (as in defining location on a stage floor), or three dimensions (necessary for describing jumps moving around a stage area).

Velocity is the rate of change of position, given by the distance traveled divided by the time required, and directed from the earlier position to the later. For instance, a dancer moving 15 feet from upstage center to downstage center in three seconds has a velocity of five feet per second towards downstage. Speed is just the magnitude of velocity, with no direction specified. The speed of that dancer would be five feet per second.

Acceleration is the rate of change of velocity, given by the difference between a later velocity and an earlier velocity, divided by the time required for the change. Note that an acceleration results from a change in the magnitude of the velocity *or* from a change in its direction. If the dancer moving downstage slows to a stop in one second, the acceleration would be five feet per second *per second*, directed *upstage*. If the dancer moving downstage *reverses* his velocity in one second, so that he is moving upstage at five feet per second, and this reversal takes one second, the acceleration is *ten* feet per second per second. Note that the speed is five feet per second before and after the acceleration, but the velocity has changed significantly. As we will see later, that change in velocity requires a force.

A special case of changing direction of velocity is motion at a constant speed in a circle. That motion is accelerated towards the center of the circle because of the constantly changing direction of velocity, even if the motion stays at a constant radius from the center.

Several useful relationships, called the kinematic equations, can be derived which relate the quantities that describe motion—distance, velocity, acceleration, and time. These relationships will allow us to relate time of flight to height of a jump, and to calculate forces required for certain movements. The simplest of these relationships is

$$s = vt,$$

where v is the average velocity during the time t taken to travel the distance s. Acceleration and velocity are related by

$$v_2 - v_1 = at,$$

where a is the average acceleration during the time t it takes to change the velocity from v_1 to v_2. Other useful relationships are:

$$v_2{}^2 - v_1{}^2 = 2as, \text{ and}$$
$$s = \frac{1}{2} at^2.$$

From this last equation we can derive a relationship between the height of a jump and the time in the air. A body acted upon by no forces other than gravity (a "free fall" condition) will accelerate downwards at a constant acceleration called g, which has a numerical value of 32 feet per second per second for *any* mass. In the above equation let t be the time during which the body is accelerating downwards from its highest point, s be the distance from the highest point to the ground, and a be the acceleration due to gravity g. Solving for t produces the equation

$$t = \sqrt{2s/g}.$$

Recognizing that s is just the height of the jump H, and that it takes the same length of time to decelerate while rising as it takes to accelerate back down to the floor, we have the equation relating the *total time* T in the air to the height of a jump:

$$T = 2\sqrt{2H/g}.$$

A jump one foot high will thus produce a time in the air of one-half second for *any* body.

The preceding discussions have dealt with *kinematics*, or relationships between the variables that describe motion. Let us turn now to *dynamics*, or analyses of motions of bodies in response to forces. Newton's three laws of motion, which he developed in the seventeenth century, form the basis of essentially all of classical dynamics. They can be stated as follows:

Newton's First Law: In the absence of any interaction with the rest of the universe, a body will either remain at rest or move continually in the same straight line with a constant velocity.

Newton's Second Law: If a body of mass m has an acceleration a, then the force acting on it is the product of the mass and its acceleration.

Newton's Third Law: If body one exerts on body two a force F_{12}, then body two exerts a force on body one of F_{21} which is equal in magnitude but exactly opposite in direction to F_{12}.

Some examples of the application of these laws may be useful. Although it usually takes some force to keep an object moving, that force is only necessary to balance frictional or drag forces that are always acting in a direction opposing the motion. A dancer moving across a floor will move in a straight line at constant speed unless there is some external force acting to change the dancer's state of motion. That force may be another dancer or a force from the floor of the kind discussed in chapter 3.

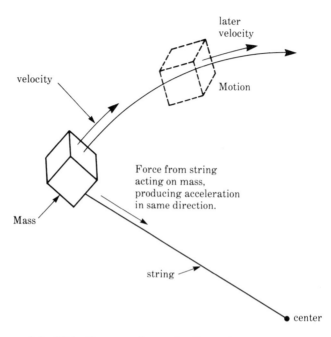

velocity

later velocity

Motion

Force from string acting on mass, producing acceleration in same direction.

Mass

string

center

Figure A-1. This diagram shows the "centripetal" force towards the center of a circular path, which keeps the mass moving in its curved path.

Circular motion is motion with a constantly changing direction, hence an acceleration; a force is necessary to change that direction. If you whirl a ball around your head on the end of a string you must exert an inward force on the string to keep the ball moving in its curved path. A dancer moving in a circular path must exert a force on the floor so that the floor exerts a force on him similar to that of the string, again directed towards the center of the circular motion.

The second law relates the magnitude of the force to the resulting acceleration. A heavy person (large weight and mass) requires a larger force to change the velocity at a certain rate than a small person. The gravitational field of the earth produces a downward vertical force on a body. This force, called the weight, is proportional to the body's mass. But since the downward force and the mass are greater for a heavy body, the downward acceleration is the same for all bodies and is called g, the acceleration due to gravity. Thus, in the absence of the force of air resistance, all objects would accelerate in free fall at the same rate.

Returning to the dancer moving in a circular path, we may state that the magnitude of horizontal force exerted by the floor on the dancer and directed towards the center of the circular path varies with the characteristics of the body and the motion. The force will be greater in proportion to the mass or weight of the body, greater for a greater speed of motion (four times as great for double the speed), and greater for a tighter or smaller-radius turn.

The third law is very important in dance, as any accelerations require forces exerted on the body, and the body is exerting equal and opposite forces on the agent of the accelerating force. That is, if a dancer wishes to accelerate toward the front of a stage, he must exert a force against the stage to the rear, and the stage will then exert the equal and opposite accelerating force on the dancer. A common question among beginning students of physics is, "How can there be any acceleration of a body if any force is balanced by an equal and opposite force?" The answer is that although the force on the body is accompanied by an equal and opposite force on the floor, there is still an unbalanced force *on the body*, causing it to accelerate.

What forces are exerted on a person standing at rest on a floor? Since the body is not accelerating, the sum of all forces acting on the body must be zero. Earth's gravity exerts a downward force which effectively acts at the center of gravity of the body, and the floor exerts a vertical upward force on the body through the feet. The body exerts an accompanying downward force on the floor.

Now consider the forces acting on the upper part of the body, above the waist. The gravitation of the earth exerts a force downward on the upper body that is equal to the weight of that portion of the body (perhaps half of the total weight). That force is balanced by an upward force exerted by the lower body on the upper body. There are no other forces acting on the upper body as a whole, so that compressive force must exist in the body at the waist, no matter how one is "placed," "pulled up," or whatever. In fact, since the internal organs of the body cannot support much compressive force, all of that force is effectively in the spine. The compressive force in the spine is a maximum at the base of the spine, because there is more of the body weight to be supported above that point than above a higher point. Of course, at the feet the entire body's weight must be supported by a compressive force exerted on what may be a small area of the foot on *demi-pointe* or *pointe*.

One of the most valuable concepts in the application of physical principles of dance involves linear and angular momentum. Momentum can be thought of as a quantity of motion, involving both the mass of a body and its velocity. The magnitude of momentum is just the product of mass and velocity, and its direction is the direction of the velocity. It can be shown that momentum is a conserved quantity—that is, the momentum of a system does not change if there are no forces acting on it, even if there are interactions or changes within the system. Suppose one person moving horizontally bounces into another. If friction is ignored, the total momentum of the two after the collision will equal the total momentum of the two before, which will be just the momentum of the first person if the second was initially at rest. One sees this in a football tackle when a runner collides with a stationary tackler, and the two bodies move after the collision with a speed less than the runner's speed before the collision. The momentum after the collision is associated with the two bodies, having more mass and therefore less speed than the first alone.

A single body may also be considered as a system composed of many parts. If the body is at rest and one part is thrust to one side, the rest of the body will recoil in the opposite direction, maintaining a zero total momentum of the system.

Rotational Mechanics

A set of laws and kinematic equations may be developed for rotational motion quite analogous to those described for linear motion in appendix A. If the letter A is an angular displacement in degrees of arc, ω (greek omega) is angular velocity in degrees per second, and α (greek alpha) is angular acceleration or the rate at which the turning speed changes, then

$$A = \omega t,$$
$$\omega_2 - \omega_1 = \alpha t,$$
$$\omega_2{}^2 - \omega_1{}^2 = 2\alpha A, \text{ and}$$
$$A = \tfrac{1}{2}\alpha t^2.$$

Recall the dancer in appendix A who was moving downstage at a velocity of five feet per second. A rotational analogue would be a dancer turning at a rate of one revolution every two seconds, for an angular velocity of 180 degrees per second. If two seconds later she is rotating at a rate of a full revolution every second, or 360 degrees per second, the angular acceleration would be the difference in those angular velocities divided by two seconds, or 90 degrees per second per second. The other two equations follow by analogy with their linear counterparts in the same way.

The rotational analogue of Newton's laws of linear motion may be expressed by substituting variables appropriate for the description of angular motion for the corresponding linear quantities, giving rise to a system of equations for rotational dynamics. In this case position, velocity, and acceleration are replaced by their angular counterparts, force is replaced by torque, which may be thought of as a turning force, and mass is replaced by moment of inertia, which is a measure of a body's inertial resistance to a change in angular motion. (See table B-1.)

Table B-1. Analogous linear and rotational quantities for kinematics and dynamics.

Quantity	Linear	Angular
Time	t	t
Position	s	A
Velocity	v	ω
Acceleration	a	α
Cause of change in motion	Force (F)	Torque (T)
Inertia	Mass (m)	Moment of Inertia (I)
Momentum	p	L

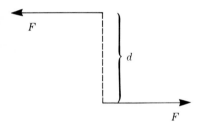

Figure B-1.
A force couple. The two forces have equal magnitudes F.

A torque arises from a force couple, which is two equal and opposite forces acting on a body, for which the lines of action of the forces are not coincident, but are parallel with some distance d between them, as in the diagram in figure B-1. The magnitude of the torque is given by the product of the force and the separation distance d, called the moment arm.

One example of a force couple is the opposite forces exerted by the two separated feet when a dancer begins a *pirouette*. Another is the opposite tangential forces exerted by the two hands of a partner when helping a dancer initiate a supported *pirouette*. If the partner's right hand pulls back and his left hand pushes forward at the waist of the partnered dancer, she will be given an angular acceleration towards the right.

The moment of inertia depends on the mass of a body and its distribution relative to the axis of rotation. A body of given mass will have a larger moment of inertia if the mass is far from the axis of rotation than if it is close. An *arabesque* position has a larger moment of inertia than a *retiré* position.

The rotational analogue of Newton's Second Law can be simply stated:

$$T = Fd = I\alpha,$$

where T is the torque whose magnitude is given by the product of the force and the separation distance for a force couple, I is the moment of inertia, and α is the angular acceleration. Clearly if the torque is zero there is no rotational acceleration. If there *is* a torque, its magnitude is large if either the force is large or the separation between the parallel lines of action of the forces is large. For instance, a *pirouette* from fifth position, for which the separation of the forces is small, is more difficult to initiate than a *pirouette* from fourth position with the feet separated. For a given torque, the angular velocity will increase rapidly if I is small, which will be true if the body's mass is compacted close to the axis of rotation. In chapter 4 we deal with torques and force couples as they apply to the initiation of *pirouettes*.

A powerful concept for dance analysis involves angular momentum. Analogous to linear momentum, angular momentum L is given by the product of the rotational inertia (moment of inertia I) and angular velocity. Thus

$$L = I\omega.$$

Angular momentum is also a conserved quantity, and L is a constant if there are no torques on a body. But

Figure B-2. The moment of inertia depends on the body configuration; it is greater when the body is extended than when it is close to the axis of rotation.

now, unlike the case of linear momentum in which the mass is almost always a constant, both the moment of inertia and the angular velocity can change. This fact has broad implications. For instance, even if there are no torques to change a dancer's angular momentum around a vertical axis, the angular *velocity* can still be changed by causing a change in the distribution of mass around the axis of rotation. An ice skater increases the rate of turn by bringing the arms and legs closer to the axis. Or a dancer doing a *grande pirouette* speeds up noticeably when the arms and legs are brought into a normal *pirouette* position. In linear motion, since it is impossible to change one's mass or weight suddenly, the linear velocity *cannot* be changed without some force being exerted on the body to change its linear momentum.

If there *is* a torque, there will generally be an angular acceleration. But because both the moment of inertia and the angular velocity can change, the dynamic equation relating torque to change in rotational motion is actually a little more subtle than that given earlier. The more general relationship is that *the torque is equal to the rate of change of angular momentum.* In the special case of constant moment of inertia, this relationship reduces to

$$T = I\alpha,$$

as stated before. But now one can see that, for a given torque, the angular acceleration will be small if I is large. This is desirable if one wants to acquire a significant angular momentum without accelerating too rapidly away from the initial position from which the accelerating torque is exerted. After the angular momentum is acquired, the moment of inertia can be decreased, thus allowing the angular velocity to increase. This process is particularly noticeable in a *pirouette en dedans* with *dégagé à la seconde,* in which the back push-off foot swings out while the body turns very little, then moves in to *pirouette* position as the body turns more rapidly. See chapter 4 for a more complete discussion of torques and *pirouettes.*

Plagenhoef has reported weights and sizes of the different body segments for both dancers and "normal" people. Some of these are reproduced in appendix C. Using these data, calculations can be made that give numerical values of moments of inertia for an average dancer in various ballet positions. Several of these are listed in appendix D. In the chapters on *pirouettes* and turns in the air (chapters 4 and 5), these moments of inertia are used to derive some useful conclusions about characteristics of turns.

Anatomical Data for a Dancer

Stanley Plagenhoef[1,2,3] has summarized the work of several investigators who determined, by measurement or modelling, the mechanical characteristics of body segments—masses, lengths, centers of gravity, and so on, for parts of the body such as forearms, head, and thighs.

Table C-1. Weights (in percentage of total body weight) and lengths (in percentage of total body height) of body segments for six female college-aged gymnasts and 35 college-aged men, after Plagenhoef.

Body Segment	Men		Women	
	Weight	Length	Weight	Length
Trunk	48.3	30.0	50.8	30.0
Head	7.1		9.4	
Thigh	10.5	23.2	8.3	24.7
Shank	4.5	24.7	5.5	25.6
Foot	1.5		1.2	
Upper arm	3.3	17.2	2.7	19.3
Forearm	1.9	15.7	1.6	16.6
Hand	0.6		0.5	

[1]Stanley Plagenhoef, *Patterns of Human Motion* (Englewood Cliffs, NJ: Prentice-Hall, 1971), chapter 3.
[2]Plagenhoef, after Dempster, W.T., "Space Requirements of the Seated Operator," *WADC Tech. Report: 55-159*, 1955.
[3]Plagenhoef, after Kjeldsen, K., "Body Segment Weights of College Women," Master's thesis, University of Massachusetts, 1969.

The data include some averages for a small group (six) of female college-aged gymnasts (presumed to be more representative of dancers than the general female population), and for 35 college-aged men. This information is summarized in table C-1.

Moments of Inertia for Various Body Configurations

There are two ways the moment of inertia is important in analyzing the dynamics of angular motion. First, for a given torque, the moment of inertia determines the change of angular momentum occurring in a particular time interval. Second, if the torque is zero (or approximately zero), angular velocity is related to the moment of inertia, which can be changed by varying the body configuration. That is, since the angular momentum is a constant when the torque is zero, a change in body position that causes the moment of inertia to double will decrease the angular velocity by one-half. (See appendix B for a more complete discussion of rotational motion.)

Several analyses require knowing the moments of inertia of the body or parts of the body in various positions, and around different axes. Before making those calculations, let us consider some simple geometrical shapes. A point mass of mass M revolving on the end of a string a distance R from the center of rotation will have a moment of inertia $I = MR^2$. Geometrical shapes in which the mass is distributed through some volume of the object may be treated as a collection of point masses, each having some small mass, and an associated effective distance from the rotation axis. Table D-1 gives some representative moments of inertia for simple geometrical shapes.

One moment of inertia we will need is that of a rigid leg oscillating around a horizontal axis through the hip joint. A rough calculation will give a good idea of the magnitude of this moment of inertia for a male of height 6 ft ½ in (about 1.84 m) and weight 159 lb (72 kg). (These figures roughly fit Sean Lavery, who is the model for the movements described in chapter 6.) The total moment of inertia of the leg will be made up of contributions from

Table D-1. Moments of inertia for some simple geometrical shapes.

Shape	Axis	Moment of Inertia
Rod, length L	Middle	$1/12\ ML^2$
	One end	$1/3\ ML^2$
	Dist. D beyond one end	$M[1/12\ L^2 + (D + L/2)^2]$
Cylinder, radius R, length L	Center axis	$1/2\ MR^2$
	Parallel edge	$3/2\ MR^2$
Sphere, radius R	Center	$2/5\ MR^2$
Circular ring, radius R	Edge, perpendicular to plane	$2\ MR^2$

the thigh, shank, and foot. Data from appendix C, plus equations for moments of inertia of uniform masses, will be used. The thigh is assumed to be a uniform rod oscillating around one end. The shank is a uniform rod oscillating around an axis $l_1 + \frac{1}{2}\ l_2$ from its center of gravity. We will assume the foot to be a point mass a

Figure D-1.
Different shapes of objects for which the moments of inertia are calculated for later use.

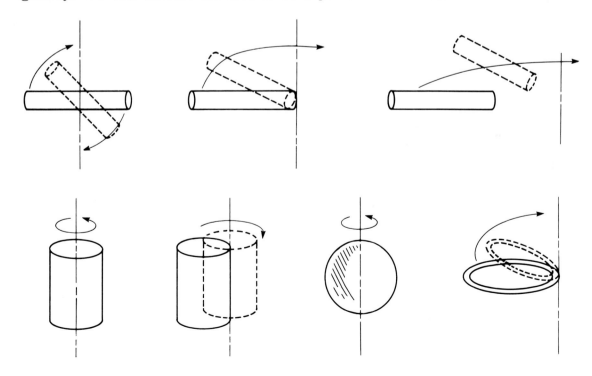

distance $l_1 + l_2$ from the axis through the hip. (The subscripts 1, 2, and 3 refer to the thigh, shank, and foot, respectively.) The total moment of inertia is then

$$I = \frac{1}{3} m_1 l_1{}^2 + m_2[\frac{1}{12} l_2{}^2 + (l_1 + \frac{1}{2} l_2)^2] + m_3(l_1 + l_2)^2.$$

Using the data for Sean, the tall dancer, and "Shorty" of chapter 6 (Sean is 15% larger than Shorty in all linear dimensions), the magnitudes of moments of inertia for the oscillating leg are

$$I = 2.75 \text{ kg-m}^2 \text{ for Sean, and}$$
$$I = 1.37 \text{ kg-m}^2 \text{ for Shorty.}$$

Now consider another important body configuration—the normal *pirouette* position. This will be idealized as a vertical body with the gesture leg in *retiré* (foot at the opposite knee), and the arms making a horizontal circle in front of the body. These calculations will be somewhat crude, but it is important to recognize two aspects of this analysis. First, bodies differ significantly, so accuracy in the calculations is not useful. Secondly, the purpose here will be to demonstrate some relative magnitudes of moments of inertia, which lead to interesting character-istics of the motions involved, rather than to development of accurate quantitative analyses.

Let us take as our example a female of height 1.6 m (5 ft 3 in) and mass 44 kg (97 lb). Assume the head and trunk form a uniform cylinder of effective radius 12 cm, rotating around its vertical axis of symmetry along with the supporting leg, having an effective average radius of 4 cm. These estimates of radius are crude, and take into account the fact that mass far from the axis is weighted more heavily than mass close to the axis. The hips, for instance, contribute a significant fraction of the moment of inertia of the rotating body, because they are generally larger in women than other parts of the body.

Adding the different contributions to the total moment of inertia, the value for this symmetric part of the body is:

$$I_1 = 1/2 \ mr^2 = 0.20 \text{ kg-m}^2,$$

using the data of appendix C and our sample female. The gesture leg forms an equilateral triangle to the side of the axis of rotation. Its contribution to the total moment of inertia I is

$$I_2 = 1/3 \, (m_1 + m_2) \, (l \cos 30°)^2 = 0.25 \text{ kg-m}^2,$$

where m_1 and m_2 are the masses of the thigh and shank, respectively. The arms form a circle of radius about 20 cm, with the axis through one edge. Their contribution is

$$I_3 = 2m_a r^2 = 0.34 \text{ kg-m}^2,$$

where m_a is the total mass of the arms. The total moment of inertia of a body b rotating in *pirouette* position is thus

$$I_b = 0.62 \text{ kg-m}^2.$$

Now for the purpose of analyzing the *fouetté* turn, consider the moment of inertia of the gesture leg alone as it is extended horizontally to the front and rotates to the side. This is effectively the same physical rotation as the oscillating leg analyzed earlier. The total I is

$$I_l = 2.55 \text{ kg-m}^2.$$

In appendix I a *fouetté* turn is analyzed numerically.

Acceleration Away From Balance

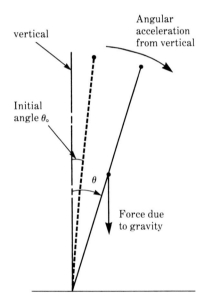

vertical

Angular
acceleration
from vertical

Initial
angle $\theta_\circ$

θ

Force due
to gravity

Figure E-1.
The toppling of a vertical
rod.

Imagine the body as an idealized stick of length L, somewhat heavier at the upper end than the lower. This stick can be balanced vertically on the floor. If it is displaced from the vertical by a small initial angle θ_0 it will start toppling, and the angle θ will increase at an accelerating rate.

The force of gravity acts on the center of gravity, and thus exerts a torque around the point of support whenever the stick is displaced from the vertical. (See figure E-1.) The equation relating the angular acceleration away from the vertical and the torque due to gravity is

$$mgR_c \sin \theta = I\alpha = mR_g{}^2\alpha,$$

where m is the mass of the body, g is the acceleration due to gravity, R_c is the distance from the point of support to the center of gravity, I is the moment of inertia of the body toppling around an axis through the point of support, R_g is the radius of gyration (defined as $\sqrt{I/m}$), and α is the toppling angular acceleration. If the angle is small, $\sin\theta$ may be replaced by θ with very little error. There results a simple differential equation which has a solution, taking into account the initial conditions,

$$\theta = \theta_0 \cosh \sqrt{gR_c/R_g{}^2}\, t,$$

where $\cosh Kt$ represents a hyperbolic cosine function of time t with constant coefficient K, which in this case has the value

$$\sqrt{gR_c/R_g{}^2}.$$

For a uniform stick of length 5 ft 10 in (or 1.78 m), the center of mass would be at the midpoint, so $R_c = 0.89$

Table E-1. Increase of angle of displacement from the vertical for tall and short toppling persons, for different initial angles of displacement.

Height	Time (seconds)	Initial Displacement Angle			
		$\frac{1}{2}°$	1°	2°	4°
5 ft 10 in	$\frac{1}{2}$	1.0°	2.1°	4.1°	8.2°
	1	3.7°	7.5°	15°	30°
	$1\frac{1}{2}$	14°	29°	57°	>60°
	2	55°	>60°	>60°	>60°
5 ft	$\frac{1}{2}$	1.1°	2.3°	4.5°	9.0°
	1	4.6°	9.1°	18°	36°
	$1\frac{1}{2}$	20°	39°	>60°	>60°
	2	>60°	>60°	>60°	>60°

m; R_g would be 1.03 m. Assuming the body is more massive at the upper end, let us increase each of these quantities arbitrarily by 15%. Thus $R_c = 1.02$ m, and $R_g = 1.18$ m. The coefficient of t in the above equation is then

$$\sqrt{gR_c/R_g^2} = 2.7/\text{sec}.$$

Note that this coefficient is greater for a small person, so that the acceleration away from vertical is, as one would expect, more rapid than for a larger person.

Table E-1 shows the angle of displacement from the vertical in degrees as it varies with time for a few initial angles of displacement for a 5 ft 10 in dancer and one 15% smaller (just under 5 ft).

Off-Balance *Pirouettes*

Suppose a dancer is off balance while performing a *pirouette*. What action is necessary in order for the dancer to regain balance?

The choice of the appropriate technique of analysis depends on the magnitude of spinning angular momentum L. If this is not very large, then the effects of rotation can be ignored, and the process of restoring balance can be analyzed as if the dancer were not rotating but just poised above the supporting point. If the spinning angular momentum *is* large, then the motion and its analysis are more complicated. The turning dancer would have to be treated like a spinning top (or gyroscope), with the possibility of precession of the rotation axis (the wobbling of the axis of a top if it is off balance).

In order to make a judgment about the magnitude of the spinning angular momentum, that L must be compared with the toppling angular momentum produced by the torque due to gravity acting on the unbalanced body. This torque is given in appendix E as

$$T = mgR_c \sin \theta,$$

where m is the mass of the body, g is the acceleration due to gravity, R_c is the height to the center of gravity, and θ is the angle of lean of the body from the vertical. In appendix B it was pointed out that torque equals the rate of change of angular momentum, so that a change in angular momentum occurring in a time Δt is given by

$$\Delta L = (mgR_c \sin \theta)\Delta t.$$

If the body spins through many revolutions while the ΔL causes a small change in direction of the almost-vertical spinning L, then precession results.

Let us estimate some numerical values of the quantities involved. Assume a female dancer of mass 50 kg (110 lb), height 1.7 m (5 ft 7 in), rotating in normal *pirouette* position at an angular velocity of two revolutions per second (12.6 rad/sec). As shown in appendix D, her moment of inertia will be about 0.7 kg-m². Her angular momentum of spin will then be

$$L = I\omega = (0.7)\,(12.6) = 8.8 \text{ kg-m}^2/\text{s}.$$

Now consider the toppling. The dancer's center of gravity is about 1.0 m above the floor. Suppose the angle of displacement from the vertical is 2°. (Ignoring the rotating motion, that angle would increase to about 4° after one-half second.) The torque is then 17 kg-m/s², giving rise to a change of angular momentum of 8.5 kg-m²/s in the one-half second it takes to complete one revolution of the *pirouette.*

It appears that the condition for precession mentioned earlier is *not* met; that is, the change in angular momentum occurring while the body is turning through many revolutions is *not small* compared to the spin angular momentum, and the rotation can be ignored. Of course if the angle of displacement is significantly smaller than 2°, or if the turn rate is greater, the rotation *would* be important. In that case, the rotation would actually *help* a dancer maintain balance, for the same reason a top topples more slowly when spinning than when not spinning. But in most cases the adjustments in balance must be made as if the angular momentum of rotation could be ignored.

Arabesque Turn Analysis

One potential problem in performing an *arabesque* turn is the "drooping leg syndrome." The gesture leg, which is supposed to be extended roughly horizontally to the rear, tends to descend during the turn. The moment of inertia of the rotating body decreases as the leg's mass is brought closer to the axis of rotation, which allows the angular velocity to increase. The centrifugal force tending to throw the gesture leg back out to the rear then increases, giving rise to an oscillation of the leg up and down.

This problem was described in chapter 4, and the result of a detailed analysis was mentioned indicating that the period of oscillation of the leg may be close to the period of rotation, making the problem particularly insidious. The more detailed analysis will now be described.

The body is assumed to consist of three main body parts, as shown in the diagram of figure G-1. The effect of the arms in contributing to the moment of inertia will be ignored, because they are so light; the contribution of the supporting leg will be ignored because its mass is concentrated so close to the axis of rotation. The axis of rotation will be assumed to lie in a vertical line along the edge of the cylindrical torso and head. We will assume a female of height 5 ft 3 in (1.60 m), weight 97 lb (44 kg), and effective radius of the torso 12 cm. The other masses and body segment lengths are taken from appendix C.

The total moment of inertia of a cylinder rotating around an axis along the edge is

$$I_b = 3/2 \ M_b \ r^2 = 0.66 \ \text{kg-m}^2.$$

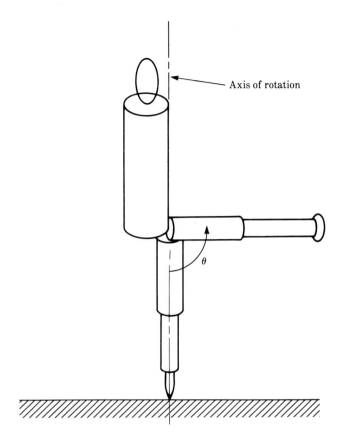

Axis of rotation

Figure G-1.
Idealized body model for the
arabesque turn analysis.

The moment of inertia of the gesture leg making an angle
θ with the vertical is

$$I_l = I_o \sin^2 \theta,$$

where $I_o = 1.44$ kg-m^2.

The effect of the centrifugal force on the leg can be treated as a torque around a horizontal axis through the hip, tending to increase the angle θ. This torque is proportional to the square of the angular velocity ω, and is given numerically (after integrating over the length of the leg and substituting assumed masses and lengths) as

$$T_1 = (1.44 \text{ kg-m}^2) \, \omega^2 \sin \theta \cos \theta.$$

The torque tending to decrease θ (lower the leg) is due to gravity acting on the center of gravity of the leg, and is given by

$$T_2 = (25.5 \text{ kg-m}^2/\text{s}^2) \sin \theta.$$

The total torque on the leg tending to increase its angle with the vertical is thus, in standard meter-kilogram-second units,

$$T = 1.44 \; \omega^2 \sin \theta \cos \theta - 25.5 \sin \theta.$$

The angular momentum of the rotating body will be assumed constant (no accelerating or retarding torques between the supporting foot and the floor). What is this angular momentum? Let us choose a rotation rate of 0.8 revolutions per second, with the leg at the equilibrium angle for that rotation rate, such that the dancer is exerting no torque in the hip to support the leg. (This is artificial, since most dancers *will* exert a torque to help support the leg. That torque will be taken into account later as a perturbing factor in the simpler analysis.)

The equilibrium angle can be found by setting the total torque in the above equation to zero and finding the θ that corresponds to the assumed value of ω. The result is

$$\theta_0 = 45°.$$

Now with that θ the total moment of inertia can be found from the first equation, and the angular momentum is

$$L = 6.95 \text{ kg-m}^2/\text{s}.$$

If this angular momentum is a constant even when the angle θ and the rotation rate change, we can use that fact to eliminate ω from the equation for total torque. The angular velocity is given by

$$\omega = L/I = \frac{6.95}{I_b + I_o \sin^2 \theta}$$

$$= \frac{4.84}{0.46 + \sin^2 \theta}.$$

Now we can construct an expression for the torque tending to change the leg angle θ in terms of just one variable, θ. Since torque is the product of the moment of inertia of the leg around the horizontal hip axis and the angular acceleration α of the leg around that axis, we have a final expression,

$$1.44 \quad \alpha = 1.44 \left[\frac{4.84}{0.46 + \sin^2\theta} \right]^2 \sin\theta \cos\theta - 25.5 \sin\theta.$$

This is a non-trivial differential equation, which can be solved by assuming that the change of θ from θ_0 is small. The numerical result of this solution is that the frequency of oscillation is about 1.1 cycles per second. This frequency is close enough to the turn rate of 0.8 revolutions per second that, with the significant uncertainties in the analysis, the two may be equal, giving rise to a "resonance" in which the leg undergoes one up–down–up oscillation while the body turns one complete turn. There is probably a mental reinforcement for an oscillation that involves a slowing of the body's rotation each time the dancer is facing the original direction. This reinforcement would be particularly strong if the head is spotting to that direction once each revolution also.

Now suppose the cavalier assumption about the lack of torque from the hip is reconsidered. Suppose the hip exerts a constant lifting torque such that the equilibrium angle of the leg is increased to 75° from the vertical. The torque necessary to accomplish that more nearly horizontal *arabesque* position can be calculated, and has a numerical value of

$$T_H = 15.6 \text{ kg-m}^2/\text{s}^2.$$

The total constant angular momentum is greater in this case, since the leg is extended farther from the axis of rotation. The relationship between the angular acceleration of the leg around the hip joint and the angle θ must take into account the additional hip torque. A solution of the revised equation produces the result that the oscillation frequency is 0.9 cycles per second, a bit slower than for oscillations around the lower angle of 45°. In fact, this oscillation frequency is even closer to the frequency of rotation, implying an even closer coupling between the rotation and the oscillating leg.

Again the result is important in that the natural tendency to slow the turn, or pause, after each revolution is enhanced by the "drooping leg syndrome" in which the leg is high and the rotation slow; then the leg descends, speeding the turn, then rises again after about one revolution to slow the turn when the body again is facing the original direction. The fact that the movement is performed without the culprit leg in sight of the dancer makes it difficult to correct this fault which has such a negative effect on the aesthetic line of the *arabesque* position during the turn.

Quantitative Analysis of the *Grande Pirouette*

The *grande pirouette* is a turn on one supporting leg with the gesture leg extended horizontally to the side (second position *en l'air*). A detailed analysis is quite involved, even when several simplifying assumptions are made.[1] The results of the analysis will be outlined here.

Assume the body can be represented by two legs, each of mass m and length l (and negligible thickness), plus the remainder of the body, of mass M, effective length L, symmetric around the longitudinal axis. The legs consist of a thigh of length $1/2\ l$ and mass $2/3\ m$, and a shank and foot of length $1/2\ l$ and mass $1/3\ m$. (These assumptions are within a few percent of data on appropriate human bodies given by Plagenhoef, and are described in appendix C.) Leg number 1, the supporting leg, makes an angle θ with the vertical; leg number 2, the gesture leg, is horizontal; the remainder of the body is effectively vertical. (See figure H-1.)

Now the question is whether there is a difference in the angle θ for static equilibrium and for the case where the body is rotating about the vertical axis.

STATIC EQUILIBRIUM

The condition for static equilibrium is that the torques about the supporting point (supporting foot on the floor) must add to zero. These torques are due to gravity acting downward on the center of gravity of each of the body segments. Let us first find the position of the center of gravity for each of the three segments in the idealized model of the body. Simple calculations show that the center

[1]The mathematical details will be furnished by the author on request.

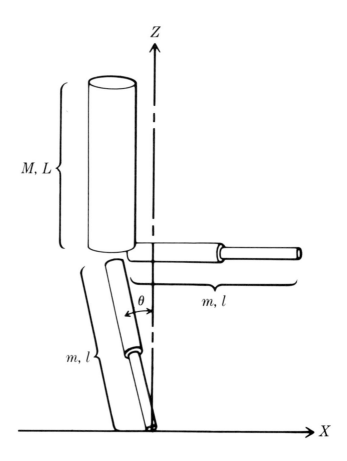

Figure H-1.
Idealized body model for the
grande pirouette analysis.

of gravity of the idealized leg is seven-twelfths of the total leg length from the foot end, or five-twelfths of the leg length from the hip. The center of gravity of the remainder of the body will be assumed to be in the center of the cylinder, since only its horizontal position is important for the analysis.

The total torque acting in a clockwise direction around the supporting foot is now given by

$$T = -mg(\tfrac{7}{12}l \sin \theta) - Mg \, l \sin \theta + mg(\tfrac{5}{12}l - l\sin\theta).$$

DYNAMIC EQUILIBRIUM

Assume the axis of rotation is vertical. For an object that is symmetric around the vertical axis, that axis would be a "principal axis," and the angular momentum could also be considered to have only a vertical component. But since the body in *grande pirouette* position is clearly not symmetric, the vector representing the angular momentum will not be vertical. (In physics terms, the inertia tensor relating angular velocity to angular momentum will have off-diagonal elements.)

Since the angular momentum is not vertical, it must precess around the vertical axis as the body rotates, forming a cone with the apex at the supporting point. But the angular momentum can only change if there is a torque acting on the body. Since the only source of torque for a freely rotating body is gravity, we conclude that the condition derived for static balance must *not* be met, so that in fact there *is* a net torque just sufficient to produce the rate of change of angular momentum giving rise to the precession.

In order to find the non-vertical component of the angular momentum, it is necessary to find the elements of the inertia tensor for each of the rotating body segments. It can be shown that the magnitude of torque needed is

$$N = \omega^2 I_{xz},$$

where I_{xz} is the xz element of the inertia tensor. That torque is then equated to the torque equation used for static equilibrium, recognizing now that that torque will not be zero, and the angle will not be 4.4°. The result of the calculation is that the angle is in fact about 3.5° for a rotation rate of one revolution per second. The effect will of course be stronger for a faster turn.

Thus when the body is rotating, a small correction must be made in the angle the supporting leg makes with the vertical, shifting the body towards the extended gesture leg. That is, the total body center of gravity must be displaced slightly to the right of the vertical axis through the supporting point in figure H-1. As the turn slows, the effect diminishes, and the center of gravity must be shifted back towards the vertical line through the supporting foot.

Quantitative Analysis of the *Fouetté* Turn

The *fouetté* turn is described on pp. 61-64. The moments of inertia necessary for analyzing this movement quantitatively were calculated in appendix D for a female dancer of height 1.6 m (5 ft 3 in) and mass 44 kg (97 lb).

Assume that the torque between the supporting foot and the floor is zero, so the body will coast in its rotating motion with constant angular momentum. The mechanical process in the *fouetté* turn involves a transfer of angular momentum between the whole rotating body during the turn and the gesture leg alone when the body is temporarily stationary *en face*. This constant angular momentum can be expressed as

$$L = I_b\,\omega_b = I_l\omega_l,$$

where I_b and ω_b are the moment of inertia and angular velocity of the whole body in *pirouette* position, and I_l and ω_b are the moment of inertia and angular velocity of the whole body in *pirouette* position, and I_l and ω_l are those quantities for the extended leg alone. If ω_b is about 12.6 rad/sec (2.0 revolutions per second in the *pirouette*), then, using the moments of inertia from appendix D,

$$(0.62)\,(12.6) = (2.55)\,(\omega_l)$$
$$= 3.05 \text{ rad/sec}\,(\omega_l) = 0.49 \text{ rev/sec.}$$

Thus the leg alone will rotate around the vertical body axis at a rate of about one-half revolution per second, which means that the one-quarter revolution needed to move the leg from front to side will occupy about one-half second.

Given the approximations used in the model for this *fouetté* turn, the time required to complete each turn (one-half second at a two-revolution-per-second rate) is equal to the time during which the body is stationary while the gesture leg rotates through its quarter turn from front to side.

Balance in Pose with Partner

In chapter 7 a situation was discussed in which the female dancer is balanced in *attitude derrière*, with support both from her supporting foot and from contact between her right hand and her partner's right hand. If she is slightly off balance she can use the contact with her partner to correct the problem in one of two ways. She can exert a *force* against his hand in the direction necessary to shift her center of gravity back to a location directly above her supporting foot, or she can exert a *torque* against his hand to accomplish the same aim. The first technique can result in an unwanted twist of her body away from her partner; the second technique avoids that problem.

In order to examine this situation in more detail, imagine the woman's body forming a vertical plane with the center of gravity almost directly above the supporting foot (point A in the diagram shown in figure J-1, which is looking down from above, as is the photograph in figure J-2). If the center of gravity is displaced slightly transverse to the plane of the body (X in the diagram), the hand at point B must exert a force in the same transverse direction in order for the reaction force on her body to return her center of gravity to the balance position on the axis through A. But clearly that net force also results in a torque around the vertical axis at A, tending to rotate the whole body in a clockwise direction when seen from above.

In figure J-3 the alternative action is shown, in which the woman's hand exerts a torque around the hand axis B, represented by the forces F_1 and F_2 and separation d. If F_1 and F_2 are approximately equal, they represent a force couple, and the reaction forces of the partner's hand against hers will cause her body to tend to rotate in a counterclockwise direction *around the axis* B. This

Figure J-1.
Lateral force exerted at the supporting hand in a supported *attitude derrière* (top view).

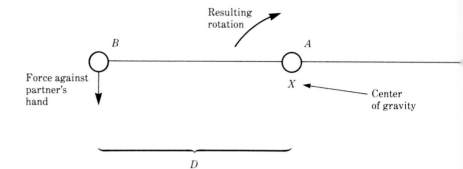

Figure J-2.
Supported *attitude derrière* viewed from above, as in the diagrams in figures J-1 and J-3.

movement will tend to return the center of gravity back to its balance location on the vertical line through A. But now if F_1 is slightly greater than F_2, the torque around A can be made equal to zero, thus allowing for a movement that restores the body to balance *without* causing the potentially disastrous twist around the A axis.

Mathematically, suppose the center of gravity of the female dancer of the size described in appendix C is displaced from balance by 1.0 cm. If her center of gravity is about 1.1 m above the ground, this displacement represents an angle of about 1/2° from the vertical. Now

APPENDIX J:
BALANCE IN POSE WITH PARTNER

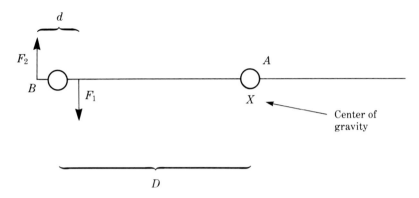

Figure J-3. Torque rather than lateral force exerted at the supporting hand in a supported *attitude derrière*.

suppose a lateral *force* is exerted against the partner's hand just sufficient to counteract the "toppling" effect of gravity. Although some of the lateral force from the hand will be translated into a lateral force at the non-slipping supporting foot, let us assume for crude calculations that all of the hand force appears as a force on the center of gravity. If the distance D in figure J-1 is also 1.1 m, the force required will be given by

$$F = mg \tan (1/2°) = 3.76 \text{ Newtons} = 0.85 \text{ lb.}$$

This magnitude of force at a distance of 1.1 m produces a torque of

$$T = 4.14 \text{ N-m}$$

around axis A. Given the moment of inertia calculated in appendix G for the *arabesque* turn, the resulting angular acceleration would be

$$\alpha = T/I = 4.14 \text{ N-m}/2.09 \text{ kg-m}^2 = 1.98 \text{ s}^{-2}.$$

This angular acceleration would twist the body through an angle of 14° around axis A in just one-half second!

Now suppose the *torque* at the hand contact is exerted instead. This torque must be equal to 4.14 N-m as before. But now the torque is exerted by a force couple of separation about 10 cm at the hand. The average of the two forces at the hand must then be about 41 N or 9.3 lb. In order to maintain a zero twisting torque around A, F_1 must be greater than F_2 by an amount given by the following equation:

$$T_A = F_1(D - d/2) - F_2(D + d/2)$$
$$= (F_1 - F_2)D - (F_1 + F_2)d/2 = 0.$$

Since T_B, the torque around the axis B, is given by

$$T_B = (F_1 + F_2)d/2,$$

the resulting equation

$$F_1 - F_2 = T_B/D = 3.76 \text{ N} = 0.85 \text{ lb}$$

gives the difference in force. Thus the hand must exert a force couple with the forces being about 9 lb separated by a distance of about 10 cm, but the force F_1 is about 10% greater than F_2 in order to prevent the twist around the A axis.

The qualitative aspects of these results, and their implications for the dancers, are discussed in chapter 7.

APPENDIX J:
BALANCE IN POSE WITH
PARTNER

Glossary of Dance Terms Used in This Book

ADAGIO: As in music, a slow tempo: a dance in a slow tempo. *Adagios* in ballets are often performed by partners. *Adagio* sections of dance classes are done in a slow tempo.

ALLEGRO: Dancing that is lively and fast, in comparison to *adagio*.

ARABESQUE: Set pose. In the most common form of *arabesque*, the dancer stands on one leg, with the other leg fully extended to the rear.

ASSEMBLÉ: Literally, together. A jump from one foot to two feet, ending in fifth position, with the feet "assembling," or coming together, in the air.

ATTITUDE: A pose similar to the *arabesque*, but with the raised leg bent. An *attitude en avant* is a similar position but with a bent leg raised to the front.

BARRE: The horizontal bar used by dancers for support and balance in the early part of a ballet class.

BATTEMENT: A beating movement of the legs.

CABRIOLE: A jump in which the legs beat together while in the air. The gesture leg leaves the supporting leg in a kick to any direction; the supporting leg rises to beat against it and then returns to the floor.

CHASSÉ: Literally, chased. A sliding step.

COUPÉ: A movement in which one foot "cuts" in to the ankle of the supporting leg. In recent use the *coupé position* is a standing position with one foot at the ankle of the other leg.

DÉGAGÉ: Literally, disengaged. A small kicking movement in place.

DEMI-FOUETTÉ: A half turn in which the gesture leg kicks to the front or back, then the body turns through an angle of 180° while leaving the gesture leg pointed in its original direction. The movement may be performed as a jump or with the supporting leg remaining on the floor.

DEMI-PLIÉ: A shallow plié, in which the heels remain on the floor.

DEMI-POINTE: Standing on a foot pointed except for the toes, which are flat on the floor.

DERRIÈRE: To the rear.

DEVANT: In front.

DÉVELOPPÉ: Literally, developed or unfolded. A gradual unfolding of the leg as it rises from the floor and is extended fully in the air. As it is raised, the foot passes the knee of the supporting leg.

EN AVANT: Forward.

EN DEDANS: Inward. Specifically, a turn towards the supporting leg.

EN DEHORS: Outside. Specifically, a turn away from the supporting leg.

EN FACE: Facing front, or towards the audience.

EN L'AIR: Aloft, as in *tour en l'air*, a turn in the air.

ENTRECHAT: A beating step of elevation in which the dancer leaps straight into the air and crosses his feet a number of times, making a weaving motion in the air. The term *entrechat* is compounded with numerals to indicate the number of movements of the legs. *Entrechat six*, for instance, means six movements of the legs, or three complete crossings.

FIFTH POSITION: A standing position with the feet together and turned out (pointing to the side), heel to toe and toe to heel.

FLIC-FLAC: A turning movement, generally at the barre, in which the working foot makes two inward swipes at the floor during the turn.

FOUETTÉ EN TOURNANT: A turn in which a whipping motion of the free leg propels the dancer around the supporting leg.

GLISSADE: A gliding movement from fifth position to an open position and back to fifth position.

GRAND: Large, as in *grand jeté*, a large jump.

JETE: A jump in which the weight of the body is thrown from one foot to the other.

MANÈGE: A circular series of turns; literally a merry-go-round.

PAS DE BOURRÉE: A three-step sequence which reverses the positions of the feet from front to back.

PAS DE DEUX: A dance for two people.

PENCHÉ: Leaning, usually to the front.

PIROUETTE: A complete turn of the body on one foot.

PLIÉ: Lowering of the body by bending the knees.

POINTE: "On *pointe*" is dancing on the toes.

QUATRE: Four.

RELEVÉ: The raising of the body onto *pointe* or *demi-pointe.*

RETIRÉ: A standing position in which one foot is at the knee of the supporting leg.

SAUTÉ: Jump.

SECOND POSITION: A standing position facing front with the feet spread apart to the side.

SECONDE: Second, as in *à la seconde,* the leg extended to the side in second position.

TOMBÉ: A lunge to the front or side.

TOURNANT: Turning.

TOUR: A turn.

Glossary of Physics Terms Used in This Book

ACCELERATION: Rate of change of velocity.

ANGULAR MOMENTUM: "Quantity of angular motion"; the product of the moment of inertia and the angular velocity.

ANGULAR VELOCITY: Rate of change of angular position.

ANGULAR ACCELERATION: Rate of change of angular velocity.

AXIS OF ROTATION: Line around which a body rotates. Parts of the body that lie on the axis of rotation do not change position as the body rotates.

CENTER OF GRAVITY: Point at which the gravitational force on a body may be considered to act.

FORCE: The magnitude and direction of "push." The force on a body determines its rate of change of momentum.

FORCE COUPLE: A pair of equal forces acting in opposite directions along parallel lines. A force couple produces a torque on an object with no net force on it.

MASS: The inertial resistance to a change in linear motion. A large mass will accelerate less in response to a given force than a small mass.

MOMENT OF INERTIA: The inertial resistance to a change in rotational motion. A body with large moment of inertia will undergo a smaller angular acceleration in response to a given torque than a body with small moment of inertia. The moment of inertia depends both on the magnitude of mass of a body and on how that mass is distributed relative to the axis of rotation, with a larger moment of inertia for mass distributed far from the axis.

MOMENTUM: The "quantity of motion," given by the product of the mass and the velocity of a body.

PRECESSION: The "wobbling" of the axis of rotation around the vertical orientation, as a spinning top wobbles while it slows down.

RESONANCE: A phenomenon whereby an oscillating force has the same frequency as a natural frequency of oscillation of a system, allowing the response of the system to the force to grow to a large magnitude. An example is a person pushing a child in a swing, in which the amplitude of oscillation grows because the pushing force has the same timing as the natural timing of the swing.

SPEED: The magnitude of the velocity, ignoring direction.

TORQUE: "Turning force." The magnitude of torque determines the rate of change of angular momentum. A pure torque arises from a force couple defined above. The magnitude of torque for a force couple consisting of two anti-parallel forces F separated by a distance D is just F times D.

VELOCITY: Rate of change of position, with magnitude and direction both specified. Velocity and speed are often used interchangeably in everyday speech.

WEIGHT: The total force of gravity on a body. Mass and weight are often used interchangeably in everyday speech, and in fact are proportional to each other in the gravitational field of the earth.

Index

Acceleration, angular, 13–14, 127–31, 138–39

Acceleration, horizontal, 17–19, 26–31, 88–89, 105, 121–25

Acceleration, vertical, 32–33, 40, 122–23

Adagio movements, 83, 90, 92

Allegro movements, 31, 83

Arabesque, 11–12

Arabesque turn, 45, 54–59, 142–46

Assemblé, 77–78

Attitude, 101–104, 151–54

Balance, 11–24, 59–61, 104–105, 138–39, 140–42, 147–49

Balance, with partner, 101–103, 106–109, 151–54

Barre, 104–105

Beats, 87–88; see also *Entrechats*

Center of force, 13–15, 26–27

Center of gravity, 125, 138

Central Pennsylvania Youth Ballet, xiv

Centrifugal force and acceleration, 56–58, 142–43

Complementarity Principle, 4

Curved path motion, 25, 29–31, 124

Dégagé, 28, 54, 66, 130

Demi-fouetté, 69, 73–74

Drooping leg, 56–59, 142–46

Dynamics, 121

Energy, 37, 87–88, 92*t*

Entrechats, 87–88, 92*t*

Finger turn, 111–13

Flic-flac, 105

"Floating" illusion, 34–36

Floor, 39–42

Force, 123–25

Force couple, 48, 79, 128–29, 151–54; see also Torque

Fouetté en tournant (*fouetté* turns), 45, 46–47, 61–64, 105, 150

Friction, 17, 21, 33, 39–42, 50, 88–90, 106–108

Grand battement, 3, 56

Grand jeté, 25, 34–39

Grande pirouette, 59–61, 147–49

Height of jump, 31–33, 34, 39–40, 122–23

Illusion, 1, 7, 34–36, 51, 72–73, 80

Kinematics, 121–23

Lifts, 97–100

Manège, 30–31

Mass, 123–26

Mechanics, 121

Moment of inertia, 7, 51, 54–56, 58, 64, 72–77, 88–92*t*, 127–31, 134–37, 142–44

Momentum, angular, 49–50, 51–59, 61–65, 71–75, 78, 110–12, 128–30, 140–41, 144, 148–49, 150

Momentum, linear, 126

Muscle force, 85–88, 90, 92*t*, 99

Newton, Isaac, 8, 26, 47, 123, 127–28

Oscillation, 56–59, 142–46

Penché, 22

Photography for dance, xvi, 4–5

Pirouette, 45–67, 89–90, 106–13

Pirouette, en dedans, 45, 54

Pirouette en dehors, 45, 53–55, 64, 89

Pirouettes, repeated, 64–65

Placement, 7

Plagenhoef, Stanley, 130, 132–33, 147

Plié, in jumps, 32

Pointe, 13–14, 41, 55

Precession, 19, 61, 112, 140–41

Resonance, 59, 145

Rosin, 41–42, 90

Ryman, Rhonda, 72

Saut de Basque, 69, 74–77

Saut de Basque, double, 76–77

Size of dancer, 83–93

Spotting, 49, 52–53, 55

Timing of vertical jump, 32–33

Tombé, 17, 18

Toppling, 13–15, 138–39

Torque, 46–50, 53–54, 75, 88, 92*t*, 103, 110–13, 128–31; see also Force couple

Tour en l'air, 78–79

Tour jeté, 69–74

Trajectory, 33–35

Turnout, 36–39

Velocity, angular, 51–55, 71–73, 127–31

Vertical motion, 31–33, 84–87, 122–23

Weight, 90–92

Wiley, Hannah, xiv, 74

"Wind up," 51–52